EM

Of a Shrinking Life

Robert Belenky

To
Oliver
And a new generation
of
Psychologists

Forward!

A desk. A mind. Immersed in images, memories, arguments, excuses, concerns, fearful thoughts and much about the end of the world. A private self-limited world or the actual world, the world in which we are all immersed or the world that floats in the ether, blind, unknowing, cold and indifferent, yet an irreducible, undifferentiated cinder, eternally immutable, devoid of life yet the mother of all life that always was and always will be, god's address or perhaps god itself, fearsome, omniscient, omnipotent, omnivorous. Its flesh devoured, it remains… an ember, grey, cool, empty and well used.

I am an ember.

Hebrew folksongs ripple from my computer in anticipation of Passover which as a non-observant nominal Jew is exotic in my empty domain. But the songs and the spirit are familiar.

I shall write something, anything, every day from now unto the end; silly, inconsequential, irrelevant or downright dumb though my words may be.

I shall spend no less than fifteen minutes each day on the task. That, I swear, is my solemn promise to myself. And to all of you.

Here then is my first entry:

Ah-ha!… but… you see, I have nothing to say. Nothing to report. No thoughts to share, no events to relate. A void. Nothing at all… Except this: I have just purchased an upgrade to my favorite computer writing program, Scrivener. And have spent the last hour fussing with it in an attempt to develop some facility in handling it.

So far so good. I had used an earlier version to good advantage. But getting back to it took the wind out of me and thus am I now cross-eyed-groggy.

My hope is that by pursuing a daily writing task I will, among other precious rewards, polish my relevant skills so that I will have little else to do but mindlessly pound the keys.

Okay. Here goes:

Got it. Yes. I am ready; serious about putting to paper my thoughts; my boasts, brags and proclamations about Gonzo Psychology, uninhabitable Academia and programs in the Vermont wilderness featuring vagrant dogs, cats, geese, donkeys and untethered children.

The purpose in all that I have endeavored to accomplish professionally was to snag the situation in the holy name of growth, enlightenment and human decency. (I shall eventually explain what I have in mind here.)

In these marks on paper or its electronic equivalent there will also be found forays into spouse-hood, parenthood, grand-parenthood, retirement and resurrection. It is to be spangled generously with views of post-career international adventures.

And advice on saving the world.

There is finally to be a conclusion relating my current life, my cushy decline into an old age spangled with meandering meditations, regrets, hopes... and dreams... and diminishment... and at least one dog... all culminating in the very best wishes for everyone, especially for you, dear reader.

Now I must get to work on this document. I have a deadline. I have just turned eighty-eight, you see.

Gone

I am, you see, a geezer. Shriveled. Fit for the antique shop or recycling bin, an accumulation of detritus, souvenirs of life and work, half forgotten scraps, rags, papers, notes, mountains of photographs and not a few digital recordings. I store within my system Kodacolor memories some yet vibrant, others faded in time. And dreams. Dreams, you see, are well known repositories of truth.

What to do with such stuff? Store it. Give it to the poor.

But a straightforward narrative is possible. The danger, of course, is tedium. "I did this. I did that." The first person singular announces sleep. An accountant's memory becomes an error more unforgettable than a dreamer's forgetting.

What if I allow fantasy to drift as it does in absent moments thus permitting the fingers to caress the keyboard in titillating delight while what remains of the rational self languishes in illusion… and lies where the mythical self dances wildly or wanders dumbly in a dream the meaning of which may never be known.

Oh, yes. To meld the mind with the improbable. That is where truth may be found. So it was in religion, in art, in song, in dance and in literature. Always.

Is not The Tempest but an hallucination in which Prospero evokes a magic world of beauty more real than Shakespeare's own? Isn't one more awake to sensuality in the fanciful forest of a Midsummer's Night's Dream than in the tedious real world of royalty?

I am arguing only for gentle celebration. For a mind adrift, not for madness but rather for a vacation in the nether world where warm bodies commingle with ripe minds.

It is in this way that I have authored the Milly stories[1] in which the Wonder Dog and I experience each other not so much as we do in the real world but instead as we draw upon that world to discover who we are or what we may have been and what we may yet become.

In this writing I have asked each story to emerge of its own accord in preparation for the emergence at some later moment of a sliver of meaning and perhaps even of truth.

Or not.

---

[1] Milly: My Life as a Labradoodle, Lulu Publishing Services, 2017

Finally: What, really, is the point of the exercises promoted in this document?

It is perhaps to arrive at a rationale for my professional life, warts and all. It is to derive the delight and heroics of paradise from workaday tedium, an excuse that I can present to my parents, now long deceased, for having spent my maturity in such a manner. It is a first draft of that excuse, a small child's rationale.

Oh, why did I not simply proceed to become a pedestrian shrink? A follower of Freud. Or Sullivan. Or Rogers. Or Skinner. Or Batman. Or ... a school teacher or summer camp counselor.

Or not?

Preludes

Dearest Family,

Tomorrow is my birthday. We celebrated it on Friday at Michael and Uli's. I thought then of things I wanted to say but had not yet formulated. I have been mulling them over in the days since and feel ready at last to take the plunge and try to lay them to paper.

To begin with, consider the fact that I am now officially—that is chronologically—old. Extremely old. Absurdly old. Older than my parents ever imagined becoming. Older by far than any of my ancestors.

On the other hand, I don't feel especially older than ever I was with the exception that I now need to nap every few hours. Plus I do forget things—items and tasks as well as words, mostly nouns. On the other hand, I was always a bit on the side of vagueness.

And every now and then it surprises me if in my current state I can accomplish anything at all. The other day on Caspian Lake, for example, I easily out-swam our multi-talented dog, Milly, who then insisted on using me as a raft, drawing blood on my side, arms and back in the attempt to climb up on me.

While it is true that actuarially speaking I am not long for this world, I do not yet sense that my departure is near. There remains time. A shadow of mental coherence is revealed along with some small motivation to think, to speculate and perhaps even to utter some few words of earned wisdom among treasures from which you of succeeding generations may choose. Some of these may prove useful in your own journeys on this earth and perhaps at last in the sky above.

Let us begin:

It is remarkable, isn't it?—or worrisome depending on your perspective—how character types repeat themselves in family history. My own parents, Max and Sophie, for examples, had strong, well defined personalities. They were responsible people, loving and supportive. Together we were a tiny crew, the two of them and me. Were it not for the fact that they worked long hours in their store—The Russian Yarmarka—we might easily have become far too tight an assemblage, too small; suffocating. Fortunately, there were ameliorating factors. Grandma Jenny was one. She was my mom's mother, a chubby, warm, inquisitive woman, often—and much to my amusement—falsely accused by Sophie of being a foolish gossip.

In my earliest years, that is until cousin Mimi arrived, I was Grandma Jenny's only grandchild. She babysat for me during the "Christmas Rush," the days preceding the holidays when business in the store was at it's peak. She offered me interesting sweets including her homemade honey cake and then observing me in Washington Square Park as I played with friends who happened along. It was all a fine arrangement.

The second fortunate circumstance of my early years was having been sent to progressive schools beginning with the Bank Street College Kindergarten, later to the City and Country School and finally, to the Little Red Schoolhouse which included the Elisabeth Irwin High School.

All of these institutions taken together determined my career. They were rooted in my mother's early days as arts and crafts counselor—she was first a skilled graphic artist and jewelry designer—then preschool teacher with the Ethical Culture Society.

This background on my mother's side and the consequent opportunities provided me with considerable peer interaction, vital for a child without siblings.

And so... formative for me on the one hand was education and art.

On the other it was agriculture, revolution, and from an early age scars of monstrous world events that stirred my imagination.

Dad, Maximovich (son of David), was born in 1893 during Russia's Czarist devolution. He arrived in America in 1911, became a citizen and turned to agriculture for a career—understandable for an optimistic Jewish boy from a country that barred Jews from the land. He enrolled in the Baron de Hirsch Agricultural School and later studied farm machinery at Michigan State Agricultural College.

Later still—but prior to meeting Sophie—Max became a consultant to Jewish Collective Farms in Ukraine. His work was sponsored by the American/Soviet Jewish Joint Distribution Committee, aka "Dzoint."[2]

The adventures that marked my father's history eventually became suggestive examples for my own life as well, especially when it came to career choice and an inclination to disregard convention.

There is a more to say about this. But now I must walk dear Milly. I shall leave you for an hour, then send around what I've put to paper. I'll be back as soon as I have a moment.

But one more point to make:

---

[2] https://exhibitions.yivo.org/items/show/5844?query=Iz%20mir%20fort&onlysite=4&np=26477

I am amazed at how characteristics—character types and themes—repeat themselves over the generations ... true at least in our family and probably in most, if not all, others as well.

Sophie, my mother, lives on. I see her mind in Alice as well as in those of granddaughters Sofia and Ella.

And son, Michael, is a dead ringer for my father, Max… as is grandson, Max, and his brother, Simon.

And brother Oliver is all of us. And Mary is all of them.

And she is me and each of them is us.

My God!

I suppose I am a Jew. I didn't know it until I reached maybe six or seven years. My immediate family was vague about religion and made only haphazard theological distinctions. Nonetheless we were proud to be Jewish.

As I drove my dad and mom to meet Mary's parents for the first time, Dad, raised in Czarist Russia, asked absently, "So, Bobby, tell me: Do Mary's parents drink?"

"What a dumb question, Dad!" I said. "What do you mean, 'Do her parents drink?'"

"Well," he answered with casual assurance, "all Catholics drink."

"First of all," I said, "it is not true that all Catholics drink—at least not to excess—and second, her parents are not Catholics. They are Protestant atheists of some kind."

"Protestant? Catholic?" he responded with a shrug, "What's the difference?"

There were perhaps a plurality of Jewish kids in my Deweyan, New York City, progressive school. I noticed that most of us came from single-child families. "Why," I asked my mother, "was I an only child? Why didn't you and Dad have more children?"

"Well," she said, "you see, with the rise of Hitler, we did not think it right to bring more Jewish children into this world."

What was it about the label, "Jew"? It was not at all clear to me how we were different than anyone else.

The extermination of Europe's Jewry by Hitler's forces was very much in my awareness. Especially puzzling was the acquiescence if not the active participation of many—if not most —ordinary people, Germans, Poles, Russians and others as well.

Why was that?

"Hath not a Jew eyes?" asked Shylock. "Hath not a Jew hands, organs, dimensions, senses, affections, passions; fed with the same food, hurt with the same weapons, subject to the same diseases, heal'd by the same means, warm'd and cool'd by the same winter and summer as a Christian is? If you prick us, do we not bleed? If you tickle us, do we not laugh? If you poison us, do we not die?"

At the same time, although distinctly Jewish in style and self concept, my parents were casual atheists, probably closer to the Ethical Culture Society than to any other group. My mother had in fact taught in Ethical Culture's kindergarten prior to my birth. And her own father was a witty skeptic, a learned but minimally schooled, godless man of the shtetl who then lived in Manhattan's Lower East Side and famously played chess on a sidewalk bench with his friend, a black man, a respected janitor.

And even my wise, paternal grandmother, whom I remember as utterly Medieval in her somber black habit, dovening as she recited prayers to her ancient god. Yet I learned from a Russian cousin some years ago that she had, in her youth, been much as we, her descendants, are today: A cheerful atheist.

My best theological role model was Cousin Boris, unmistakably gay—in every sense the word suggests—an iconoclast; a comic who had neither time nor interest in any god at all. He was a playwright and newspaper critic based in the Second Avenue Yiddish theater. He was also an excellent carpenter and bicyclist.

"Deedle-deedle-deedle," Boris sang raucously as he danced on our back porch with a Black-Eyed Susan which he called "a Cockeyed Susannah" taped to his bare chest. Perched on his bald head was a handkerchief with a knot tied at each of its four corners. I laughed so hard that my bacon, lettuce and tomato sandwich spurted out through my nose.

Later I found my favorite model for a Jewish identity: Charlie Chaplin, first in the one-reelers and finally in The Great Dictator. As hilarious as Cousin Boris, Chaplin came equipped with moral content that condemned the cruel to ridicule while celebrating the B'rer Rabbit wit, the courage and the ultimate victory of the oppressed.

The Jew, the Christian, the Muslim, the believer in Santeria and Voodoo, the humanist, the atheist, the virtuous, the humble, the devout, the loving, the just, the evil and the unformed join together in resounding chorus…

"In the mind of the universe, we are all but one." That is what I believe. That belief is my God.

Boris II

Many years later we owned a dog, a Norwegian Elkhound, whom we named after Cousin Boris. This Boris was furry. He had a tail that curled up and then down again almost touching his back. His ears stood up straight and pointed. He was spooky smart. He listened carefully to what we said. He was interested in everything. And his eyes were always bright and shiny.

Boris was a great dog. But unlike Cousin Boris, he was not funny. Not at all. This Boris was very serious. He always wanted to help. He guarded our house. He barked loudly if someone he didn't know came to the door. But he didn't bite. He never bit anyone. But he did eat some ducks over the years, raw, plus a chipmunk and a squirrel or two.

Boris was not big but he was very strong and loved to work. He was a good worker. When we went out to the woods for a picnic, he carried all of our food plus a couple of folding chairs on a wagon that he dragged behind him. And he carried our furniture and trash out afterward.

You could always rely on Boris.

But Boris was lonely. He never married. He had no children.

And there were no other dogs around to play with.

Oh, it was really worse than that. Boris once looked in the mirror and saw that his fur was grey and black.

Just then a beautiful black and yellow butterfly landed on a red rose beside him. "How beautiful that butterfly is," he said to himself. "And how ugly I am," he murmured while looking at his reflection in the pond beside him. "Oh, how I wish I were beautiful. I am but boring grey and black."

"But Boris," I said. "You are a wonderful, helpful, kind, hard-working dog. And we think you are very beautiful. And we love you."

"Grrrr," Boris said, hanging his head down low, a tear in his left eye.

Two weeks later, while in the sun by the barn door while Boris was taking his usual afternoon nap, up hopped a young lady toad.

"Good day, sweet dog," she burped most cheerfully.

Boris opened one eye. Then the other.

"You are the most beautiful animal I have ever seen," Boris softly growled. "You are green and yellow and red and have the biggest and most lovely eyes that I have ever seen."

"Thank you," she said. "And you are the handsomest dog I have ever seen. I adore furry animals who are kind and nice, have sweet voices and like to work hard."

"Let's get married!" Boris exclaimed.

Yes. Of course," she said.

And with that she jumped into his outstretched front paws as he craned his neck to gaze lovingly into her beady green eyes.

And there they remained until we called Boris into the house for dinner. "See you tomorrow," he said to his gorgeous toad. "Same time, same place."

And the next day and for many days after that, Boris could be seen stretched out in the sun by the barn with his lovely lady toad sitting comfortably in his front paws as he gazed admiringly into her beady green eyes.

We have a photograph somewhere of Boris doing exactly that.

The Village

A three-room, fourth-floor apartment on West 8th Street, Greenwich Village, New York.

My parents' store was down the block on the south side of the street. Washington Square Park was two blocks away. I played there with my friends. Every day.

My parents worked long hours in the store, originally known as the Russian Yarmarka—meaning "annual market" in its original German which then sneaked into Russian just as the German Gesuntheit found its way into English. The Yarkmarka was a constant festival of a place that offered everything from blouses to slippers to lamp shades to toys to jewelry to gossip. All very colorful.

With the advent of the Cold War, Russian items went out of favor. The business was thus reborn as "Wedding Rings, Inc." No more toys and stuff. The new incarnation was boring but useful. Friends were approaching a marriageable age.

As always—except for the Christmas rush—it was a hangout for my friends and friends of my parents. Many of the latter were garrulous salesmen, artists and insightful emigre gossips with exotic accents.

I was not a lonely child. But I was alone a lot. I would have preferred siblings. Hanging out in Washington Square was fine but not the same thing.

Washington Square. I remember sitting on a park bench with Grandma Jenny, my mom's mom. She took care of me during the Christmas Rush when my parents, working long hours in the store, were seldom available. I was maybe four or five. Courtesy the Yarmarka I pulled a Russian toy after me. It was a brightly painted wooden duck on wheels. It quaked when I pulled it. I descended from the park bench, yanked the leash and the duck followed me. "Waak! Waak! Waak!"

"Grandma!" I said. *"**Lookit!**"*

As the years passed, my life tilted toward roller skates, stick ball, tag, fights and hanging out with friends. We constituted a generous collage of social class and political divisions although we were, you see, private school kids. But for the most part, neither elite nor affluent. Our parents tended to be artists, teachers and, like my parents, small business people. There were public school kids in the neighborhood—and, this being adjacent to New York's Little Italy, there were also kids who attended Saint Anthony's Catholic School. They reputedly hated Jews and loved Mussolini.

"Hey, Kid!" A gang of how-many-I-have-no-idea stopped us one morning on our way to school.

"You love Mussolini?"

"Well," one of us replied, "you see ...."

"You a *Jew?"*

"A Communist?!!"

"I'm gonna punch your face in!" Although that never actually happened, the possibility remained of concern.

We glanced at each other and scattered. "Those kids are Fascists!" we whispered.

But life takes surprising turns. In high school some of us walked door to door in Little Italy, distributing literature for Vito Marcantonio, Representative to the US House; a proud socialist as well as ally of then Mayor Fiorello LaGuardia who, my Grandma Jenny explained, was half Jewish.

Over the years brief conversations with some of those kids actually occurred. We even learned a few of their names and, once when I was maybe twelve or so, I walked one of their girls to St. Joseph's Academy, her school on Waverly Place. I don't remember her name.

I think she liked me. I liked her. But she made me nervous.

Once she followed me to my parents' store. I didn't invite her in. My parents would not know what to make of her. I just said, "Well, so long."

I was shy. She spoke with a New York Catholic accent; dropped her "t's."

My parents would think she was my girlfriend. She wasn't. I was way too young to have a girlfriend. But I thought about sex a lot and she made me nervous. She may have been pretty. Probably she wasn't.

I was then, as I say, maybe twelve. All girls made me nervous. Except for most of the girls in my class. We went to a private school; a "progressive" school. We were all pretty much like brothers and sisters except that when us boys hung out together, we made jokes about the girls especially those who were growing bumps on their chests.

Jokes like that made us giggle so hard we almost threw up.

Or peed in our pants.

Or something.

Bozo

One bright, light spring day, Grandma Jenny arrived at the Yarmarka with a cardboard box inside of which was a puppy—of all things. A brown and tan, fluffy, tail-wagging, cheerful puppy. "He's for you, Bobby," Grandma said. "He's your birthday present. What will you call him?"

"I will call him '*Bozo!*" I said.

I was transfixed, happy beyond words. My mother, however, was annoyed with her mother, my Grandma Jenny, as was so often the case. At such times she called grandma "foolish" and "immature."

Dad mumbled something about how it will be okay tomorrow when mom, grandma and I will take the train to the country and remain there for the summer. Dad would stay the week in the City to manage the store and then drive out to join us on Sundays.

Okay. But it ended badly.

I stood in the recently planted vegetable field. Bozo was at my feet, tale wagging, eager for fun. I reached into my pocket for a dog biscuit. I kept a supply with me at all times. I then raised the biscuit high.

"Jump, Bozo!" I said.

Bozo jumped. He snapped up the biscuit, wagged his tail and looked up at me eagerly for another go-around.

I held up a second biscuit. Bozo jumped, more excited than before. He snarfed up the biscuit and yipped his readiness for a third.

He leaped high once more but this time I inadvertently flung my left arm, the one holding the biscuit, to the side. Bozo missed his goal and bit me at in the crotch of my elbow joint instead.

I jerked my arm away. Between the two of us, Bozo and me, we managed to rip my skin and set off a small but significant torrent of blood.

I panicked and ran, crying, into the house where my mother was sorting laundry. Seeing blood, she called a neighbor. The two of them rushed me to Dr. Mollinoff who tended and bandaged the wound.

Everyone—including me—calmed down eventually.

But when my father returned the next day, he announced that Bozo was dangerous and, without hearing my side of it, impetuously drove him to the local pet store where in turn they would surely lead him to the execution chamber.

I was beside myself. Utterly inconsolable. Unforgiving of my parents. I have physical and psychological scars that remain to this day.

As a result there were no more dogs in my life until a couple of years after Mary and I married. We had two children then. I has a post-doc internship in Boston. We summered in a small cabin that we had rented in New Hampshire.

One day before driving home, I visited Boston's Angell Memorial Animal Hospital and on impulse adopted a very cute puppy, the first dog since Bozo.

What shall we name him, I asked? "Alice," said Michael then two years old. Alice was his sister, the only name he knew.

Mary and I overruled him for practical reasons. We settled on "Melanie," after the then famous child psychoanalyst, Melanie Klein.

Melanie was a great dog. She lived for sixteen years to a gracious and dignified decline and regrettable demise. She was very beautiful. We lived on Alpine Street in Cambridge. "What kind of dog is that?" people would ask. "Oh, I would say, 'that is an Alpine Shepherd.'"

One guy replied, "Oh, yes. They are very fine animals." I was embarrassed for him.

Work

Perhaps there is some value in psychotherapy. Who is to say? Surely not me, that's certain. Neither is it clear how or why I landed in such a field. Happenstance probably. In retrospect, my professional life seems to have made a promising start. And not a bad ending. My initial choice probably did make a certain amount of sense. But it may have been fate.

On the other hand, I never did become a real psychologist.

"Camp counselor" was more like it.

Okay. So, I graduated Cornell an indifferent English major. I began as a pre-med. Not that I was interested in medicine. To the contrary. I had precious little if any. But one needs work to live in this unforgiving world and I figured that doctors have an easy life and make good money.

For a time, it all went well enough. My grades were not bad and some of my courses were actually interesting. I enjoyed Romantic Poetry, for example. And Philosophy was good; better than okay.

Genetics started with promise but the class was held way too early, eight or eight-thirty am, and way far out on the Ag School's distant campus. I made it there for the first session but didn't get back again until close to the end of the semester.

"Who is that fellow giving the lecture?" I asked the guy in the seat next to mine.

"That's our professor," he answered. "But ..." I said. "Where is that other guy?"

"Oh, him? He left after the first session. Went to Europe on a research project."

Genetics wasn't for me.

There was chemistry. Inorganic was okay. Organic was, too; manageable except for the day when the instructor opined, "If you just follow directions, the experiment you are about to perform is perfectly safe."

I did exactly what he asked of us.

Yet somehow... ka-BOOM! Stuff with a pungent odor sprayed out of my jar. "I am so sorry, Sir," I stammered as students guffawed all around me.

Defeated, I sought help at the college's counseling center. "I have no idea what to major in," I explained.

They put me through several days of test-taking plus a few interviews.

"These are the results," a young fellow with horn-rimmed glasses and a white lab coat reported at the conclusion.

"Your interest and ability profiles suggest that you would do well as an English major."

"Wow!" I thought. "English! All that is required of English majors is that they loll about and read. No labs to ruin every morning and afternoon. So, that is exactly what I shall be—an English major!"

"Guess what?" I told Mr. Adams, my favorite English instructor, "I have decided to become an English major. Someday I will have a job like yours."

"Congratulations," he replied sourly. "By the way, what do you imagine my annual salary is?"

"No idea."

"Two thousand dollars," he said.

I gulped. Even then, that was miserable pocket change.

So ... my attention drifted to other possibilities. "Because this is a capitalist country," I reasoned, "I shall become a businessman."

Upon graduation, I therefore enrolled in the Columbia University's School of Business master's degree program.

After two days of class it became apparent that my professors were both tiresome and incomprehensible. And I experienced a powerful need to remain clear of my tie-and-jacket attired fellow students. Superannuated frat boys.

I never darkened that classroom again.

There were perhaps other options to explore in the World of Work. These included two days—maybe a week—in an advertising agency and a couple of weeks as copyboy with Hearst's United Press International News Service.

The UPI scene was hyperactive. People rushed hither and yon waving sheets of typed-upon paper. Shouting. Ringing, clicking, banging on keyboards. Radios. Telephones.

I gulped a sandwich lunch with an older, experienced-looking fellow. Turns out he had been doing this job for six years while at the same time working for a Ph.D. at Columbia. Brilliantly qualified, he was, but he remained a copyboy.

"Get me out of here!" I said to myself.

But before decisive action was possible, an editor nabbed me. He handed me a paper on which a name was written, an address accompanied by some guy's copy.

I nodded, "Yes, sir!"

Then glanced at the sheet. The author: Westbrook Pegler. Wow! The notorious right-wing columnist!

I trotted to the Upper West Side address. A modern elevator took me to Mr. Pegler's floor. I rang the bell.

The door swung open and there I beheld the great man himself in pajamas and bath robe. "Come on in," he said with considerable warmth. "I am Westbrook Pegler. And you are ...?"

"Bob," I gulped. "Bob Belenky."

"Ah," he said with an unmistakable gay lilt. "Belenky... Belenky. That name is so familiar. Do you perhaps have a relative in the government... or maybe the F.B.I.?"

"No, sir. I don't." The fact that he associated me with agencies that scoured the country for subversives threw me into a silent panic.

However, Mr. Pegler was disarmingly gracious. He offered me coffee and cookies and asked about my career goals. I said that I was thinking about becoming a journalist.

"Be careful," he advised. "Editors can be nasty." With that, he handed me the copy for his next column.

I thanked him. We parted. I carried his copy to the editor who nodded receipt of same.

Service

Further reflections on college life:

I was a radical then, a leftie; not a serious Marxist, the scholar immersed in literature, theory, history and slogans, songs, inspiration and organization. Unkempt. I was sympathetic to all that but was basically an unkempt kid whose instincts the further to the left one stood, the more decent—if not to say heroic, a person surely was.

And so it came to be that I devoted myself to world peace and universal betterment. I attended numerous meetings, picketed, pressed flyers in the hands of passersby and fell into lightly informed fracases with friends, acquaintances and an occasional professor—precious few of whom actually congratulated me. But the tingle of danger kept me awake and added a frisson of righteousness to my life.

College was theater. Nominal acts of morally justified rebellion were in imaginative balance with a passible, unremarkable but nonetheless enjoyable student life.

The principal venue for much of this was a huge gymnasium when, during our weekly classes in the mandatory—for freshmen and sophomores—of ROTC, the Reserve Officer's Training Corps. All male—no female—students were required to enroll in this program the goal of which was surely to compensate for the tendency toward independent thinking displayed by the occasional student.

Cornell University, it may be remembered, was a serious, universally respected, institution. But because an obscene war was then incinerating Korea, a place few of us knew anything about, the notion prevailed that we must arm ourselves to prevent a yellow-skinned horde from invading our shores. That, more more or less, was the thinking.

Neither I nor any of my friends took our war training seriously. Quite the contrary, we fought back. We viewed war as benefitting no one but munitions makers.

As we stood at nominal attention, we whispered salacious jokes about our dreary-witted military instructors on loan from the real army as we did very our best to appear as credible students of the warriors.

Our agreed-upon goal was to pass the course with as low a grade as possible. If one received an A or a B, it suggested that he was taking the nonsense seriously and might have been studying. On the other hand, an F was an unfortunate indication that the person in question was on the dim side and consequently might be required to repeat the course, an unthinkable consequence.

The aim was therefore to receive a D, a passing grade but as close to failure as possible.

I am proud to say that I obtained a C- and was heartily commended for it by my friends.

Some went further. An example was my friend George, Republican, aristocratic, witty, overweight and congenitally sloppy. George once waved his training rifle at a real army captain who screamed, "You are the worst soldier I have ever seen in my forty years in the army!"

George beamed.

Then there was Marty, skinny, stooped, brilliant and quirky; a math major. We were required every now and again to march, armed and uniformed, around campus, six abreast in one long line. In the first row was our Marty.

"Column Right!!!" the sergeant screamed.

But he misspoke. To the right was a wall of the zoology building. A big, open field was to our left, the one that the unfortunate sergeant obviously had in mind.

With the faintest smirk on his otherwise blank face, Marty, in a Chaplinesque maneuver, led the column into the wall on the right as instructed.

"You fucking idiot!" screamed the unhappy sergeant.

We all cracked up.

The sad fact was that, however unjust, a war was in fact going on and cannon fodder was needed. But neither I nor most of the people I knew were motivated to meet the demand.

What to do? Because I had no religious grounds for becoming a conscientious objector, there seemed but one option: Enroll in the voluntary sections of the ROTC program for our junior and senior years. Anyway, in two more years the war would be over, I figured.

Thus in good conscience, I applied for those additional enrollment years and looked forward to life as a second lieutenant. Unfortunately, I was turned down because of intentionally marginal ROTC grades earned during my freshman and sophomore years.

So, along with a busload of other young men, I was brought to Syracuse, New York, for a pre-induction physical. My last, hope, I reasoned, was to contact a doctor who had seen me briefly when I was seven or eight years old. He misdiagnosed me asthmatic. My parents and our family physician—dad's brother, Uncle Jack—thought it more likely that I had hay fever. I suspected that they were correct.

Nonetheless, the diagnosis had been made fairly and squarely and had duly been recorded in the doctor's notes. Asthma might now prove useful, I figured, because it could qualify as a barrier to the draft.

I contacted that physician and requested a written statement of his opinion of my condition as determined when I had seen him twelve years before. He graciously provided me with the note. "Asthma" was written prominently upon it.

I carried that document to the pre-induction physical and handed it to the fellow at the desk. Then I breezed through the examinations. At the end, the doctor in charge declared me to be in good shape, a fine physical specimen; an ideal inductee.

"But, sir," I reminded him, "No one has asked about my asthma problem. I am an asthmatic as you can see from the letter that I presented this morning. I should therefore be examined by a physician who can evaluate my condition. This must presumably be a psychiatrist because, as you are aware, asthma is in part a psychiatric illness."

The fellow in charge, a reasonable man, sent me back to the examination area, this time for an interview with a psychiatrist.

I was worried. I knew nothing about asthma, mental illness or psychiatry but could see that I had now got myself into a corner where I would be obliged to act in a manner consistent with asthma. If I made the smallest error, I would be found out. Then what? Arrest? Jail? Humiliation?

Conversation with the psychiatrist:

Doctor: So?

Me: I have asthma.

D: So what?

Me: Asthma is a psychosomatic illness that makes it impossible for me to be a soldier.

D: No it doesn't.

M: Yes it does.

D: No it doesn't.

M: Well, maybe it doesn't but I also have problems with authority.

D: Tell me about them.

M: If I don't get my way, I have a temper tantrum.

D: I think the army would do a kid like you a lot of good.

M: No! No! No! No! ....

I figured I'd blown it. But imagine my happiness when a few days later I received an official letter stating that I was to undergo a follow-up induction interview in a couple of weeks at Governor's Island in the New York City harbor. I was to be evaluated by a psychiatrist.

Now I had a new worry: As an English major, I had taken only one psych course. Consequently, I had little or no understanding of mental illness. Now I would be obliged to convince a psychiatrist that I was suffering from one. Surely I would be found to be a fraud and punished in some terrible way.

Several weeks later, I was in New York's Battery Park boarding the ferry boat to Governor's Island, shaken but with a brave but pallid face.

Governor's Island was a military base. People walked around in uniforms and the office buildings were long, white Quonset huts. I was directed to one of these and found myself in the sparsely furnished office of a lieutenant who introduced himself as a psychologist.

"I am going to administer a few simple tests to you," he explained.

The first was to draw a picture of a person. I don't remember the others.

"Therefore, my task," I reasoned to myself, "is to employ art in such a way as to demonstrate that I am too mixed up to be a soldier. How shall I proceed?"

The answer came at once. I drew a full body image of a man, naked except for tight-fitting bathing trunks on which one could plainly see the outlines of a penis.

"That might do it," I thought.

The lieutenant, making no comment, accepted the picture. He then led me to a meeting room down the hall in which on one side of a long table were seated perhaps five well uniformed and nicely decorated, square-faced officers.

"We are psychiatrists," one of them explained. "We want to ask you a few questions."

("I am done for!")

I cannot now recall what they asked. But I do remember being in a state of cold terror, certain that I would be discovered to be the fraud I surely was. I calculated that my only chance lay with the anxiety, swimming in it, luxuriating in it, magnifying it. So it was that I stammered and mumbled, sweated and gazed, alternately at my feet and the ceiling. But always avoiding their eyes.

Many questions were asked, none of which I recall.

They conferred. Then the lead psychiatrist, blank-faced, thanked and dismissed me.

I returned to New York City on the ferry, rattled but relieved and with a touch of pride in having survived the afternoon.

About a week later, I received a US government letter announcing straight out that I was not qualified to be a soldier. I had received a 4F classification. Unacceptable to the army.

I experienced unmitigated joy. But then I thought, "Maybe they know something about me that I don't know."

* * *

Some years later and after one thing or another I became a clinical psychologist. I once spotted that military psychologist at an annual professional convention. He didn't notice me; I said nothing to him.

Later still when Mary and I considered marriage, I mumbled to her, "there is something about me that you should know."

I told her the entire story. She shrugged her shoulders. And we entered into a fine and not particularly abnormal marriage now in its sixty-first year.

Woodland

My first actual job was camp counselor: Counselor in Training or "C.I.T." Volunteer. That was back in 1945, the summer that I become fourteen. I wasn't paid in U.S. currency but rather in credibility, experience and training. I was assistant to various experienced counselors.

And the following summer I was promoted to Assistant Counselor. This meant that I had some genuine responsibilities and was paid a full twenty-five dollars for the eight week session.

I returned yet again the third summer. This time I was paid a bit more and was given two responsibilities, assisting in a cabin and helping out at the waterfront.

I had two mentors, one a cabin counselor, different each year; the other, the waterfront director, a businesslike, athletic young woman.

It wasn't actually a waterfront, but rather a large outdoor swimming pool.

This was at Camp Woodland, long since defunct, run by Norman Studer, a left-winger who grew up in a Mennonite family and married a Jewish woman. Woodland was an institution solidly within the

Progressive Education tradition, indeed a leading institution. It emphasized folklore, particularly that of the Catskill Mountains in which it was embedded.

Led by resident academic folklorists and professional musicologists, campers scurried off into the surrounding hills and communities to interview people and transcribe their songs and stories about the old logging days. Bright-eyed New York City kids encountered grizzled old men and wrinkled old women who related tales, played the fiddle and sang songs from a forgotten era only some fifty years before.

"Oh, I am a poor unlucky chap.
I'm very fond of rum.
I walk the road from morn 'til night.
I ain't ashamed to bum.
"From New York unto Buffalo
I tramped it all the way.
I slept in brickyards, old log barns
Until the break of day.
"If the weather be fair,
I comb my hair
And still I didn't complain.

I got up and I heisted my turkey And I walked the road again."

Sophisticated professional folklore musicologists accompanied us. They transcribed each precious note and syllable we heard. The children thrived on the experience. There were no digital or tape recorders in those days. Cameras existed but it was the impressions engraved in our minds that really counted.

Throughout each summer we belted out old songs and danced convivial dances of that all but forgotten recent age.

And each year, in collaboration with Phoenicia, New York, our neighboring town, we produced a lively folk festival complete with old songs, and dances, both square and round. And we put together a museum of saws, hammers, drills, picks and axes, work tools of that era.

And we danced just about every week. And sang the songs and told the stories.

It was all great fun for kids and counselors alike and serious anthropological research proceeded apace. Leading folklorist Ben Botkin visited. Norman Cazden, prominent musicologist, recorded the songs, and the young Pete Seeger occasionally entertained. His father-in-law and brother-in-law were both on staff.

A remarkable place, appreciated at the time and all the more so in retrospect for its example and very existence.

Wow!... eventually I was ready for something. Anything.

Dearest Progeny...

Oh, thank you so very much. We appreciate your concerns and are pleased to know that you understand our desire still to participate in the real world as much and for as long as we reasonably can.

The family model for end-of-life care that so attracts you on our behalf may once have worked for many as surely it does today in certain places and cultures. Nonetheless, it is known for drifting more often than not across the lines that divide loving care on the one hand from constraint and downright oppression on the other.

Fortunately, it appears that you and we are agreed that a sweet spot between autonomy and support is where a reasonable person ought take aim. This requires thought and persistence on the part of both the helper and the helped. Not easy. But I suspect that our own family is close to having approached that balance.

However, we would have little interest in remaining much longer in this world if we were able neither to be of use, nor to enjoy the company of others; nor especially not to learn nor to grow. Same is likely true for most people we know. To sit around inert as lumps of clay wont do for us.

Kendal, our kindly retirement institution, resembles a well functioning traditional village in that it provides a healthy social life, culture, connections with the larger world—including Dartmouth (a nice little university); assistance when needed

and the opportunity to help others as they help us and in turn to enrich their lives as they do ours. Not bad. Interesting note: Its benefits—when you come down to it—are not unlike those in the best of old fashioned societies.

This is not to say that we reject you neither do we abandon our biological families nor our in-laws. It is rather that in our cozy institution we find ourselves free to enjoy your company in this supportive, minimally stressful environment that is our fortunate turf.

When we at last are obliged to depart this vale of tears, we hope we will be remembered as we were at our more or less coherent and loving.

Meanwhile, having just celebrated my eighty-eighth birthday, I feel that I have a builtin, reasonable deadline for completing this rambling book.

Blinkers

Starting in my high school senior year and for each of the four subsequent summers, I took camp-counselor jobs. After three at Woodland, I decided to try someplace else. I selected "Wo-Chi-Ca." Sounds like a Native American name. Actually, it stands for "Workers' Children's Camps," a cool leftie reference. Before my time it was said that a red flag was raised each morning.

The chorus of a camp song went like this:

> *"Pick and spade, pick and spade.*
> *"We are Tito's Youth Brigade."*

Inspiring to be sure, but Yugoslavia seemed remote; anyway, I missed the fun-loving, earth-bound folkloric research scene at Woodland. And ... I was prepared to explore variations on the camping theme. I wanted to stretch myself.

And so, one day I dropped into the New York State Employment Office—Summer Section, to poke around and learn what jobs they might have on file.

A position that had immediate appeal was guide on the tour boat that circled Manhattan Island. That was right up my alley. I spoke to the guy at their booth but was discouraged because of my lack of relevant experience.

With a shrug, I wandered over to the Summer Camps desk. I explained that I was a waterfront expert. There were in fact a few openings. One was at a Jewish day camp. Okay... but perhaps a bit too conventional, possibly boring.

I was about to head to another desk when a guy with quasi-military bearing showed up and shook my hand. He explained that he was the new director of "Camp Marcella," otherwise known as The New Jersey Camp for Blind Children. It was sponsored by the Education Department of the New Jersey State Commission for the Blind.

He needed a Waterfront Director for the coming summer.

Wow! A fascinating challenge.

I introduced myself.

"Fred Sigafoos, US Navy, Retired," he replied.

A fine fellow, pleasant smile, a bit more on the military side than what I was used to. But, hey!

Pending a look at my reference file, I was hired. Right then and there. On the spot.

Thus began three summers of teaching blind and deaf-blind children to swim, paddle a canoe and row a boat.

I discovered at once that very first summer, how rugged some of those blind kids were. Remarkably so.

It was actually a bifurcated population. Many kids were passive, withdrawn and given to starring at television—on a cheap set lacking a video tube. But other kids were on the wild side, risk takers, tormenters, challengers and deniers, temporarily freed from the hinderance of vision to celebrate their skill and daring at negotiating the sighted world.

Never shall I forget ten-year-old, red-headed, glass-eyed Ralphie,[3] as he galloped full speed down the hill in the center of the campus—all the while screaming,

"Outta my way, Blinker coming!"

(Blinker: Blind slang for blind person.)

Then there was Joey, also about ten, a sightless Huck Finn.

Joey discovered that he was immune to poison ivy, a major New Jersey crop. Eyeless by virtue of cancer, Joey learned to detect the leaf by touch alone. His signature delinquent act was to harvest it from behind his cabin and rub it on the toilet seats of the girls' dorm.

---

[3] Real names of campers not used.

Oh, them were the days!

Alan Sussman, my buddy who I haven't seen since then, was a contrarian arts and crafts counselor. He and I pretty much ran the camp that summer. And the subsequent two as well.

We sponsored evenings of goofy songs, dances and pointless games. These took place in a weekly evening session we called, "Destructive Recreation."

Alan's theory—to which I adhered—was that blind kids living at home in the sighted world tended to be overprotected, pitied, ignored and closeted. We at Camp Marcella, on the other hand, operated under the principle that camp was a proper, indeed a necessary, zone for cutting loose, for irrepressible spirits and to frolic in witty and relatively harmless delinquency. In all of this we were successful.

Ninety percent theater, nothing regrettable occurred. And the kids, utterly turned on, loved it.

I ran the waterfront in much the same spirit.

Our blind kids varied in their capacity to deal with the world. Some were maudlin, overweight, passive recipients of good will and tolerant of sighted ignorance and insensitivity. Others battled the limitations of their handicap along with the ignorance and condescensions of the sighted world. This they did with wit, theatrics, indignation and fury—sometimes overt but more often internalized.

All this came into focus one day when members of the Boy Scout camp from down the road came for a visit. They sauntered down to the waterfront to observe our kids splashing around.

"Blind children in the water! Just imagine! How wonderful!"

The next day we received a phone call from the Scout leader. Impressed with our sightless inhabitants, he suggested a day of swimming events for the two camps.

Marcella campers considered this to be a fine idea. Older kids went into training, swimming a few practice laps at every opportunity.

The great day arrived. The Boy Scouts were polite but our older kids were quick to sniff the familiar odor of condescension in the air.

The events consisted of four free-style races, each for a different age group.

An announcer, not easy to hear over the cheering, described what was going on.

Soon, remarkably, VICTORY! arrived. The celebrated Blinkers of Marcella won three out of the four races!

[Resounding, operatic cheers!]

Danny, a chubby ten year old whose main activity during the fall, winter and spring involved sitting in front of a television set that featured a blacked-out screen from which spewed soporific soap operas, averred:

"Us Blinkers, we showed those Boy Scouts a thing or two!"

"What is biggest in Egypt?" I asked arts and crafts counselor, Alan.

"De Nile," he replied.

"Precisely," I said.

Some of our campers were both blind and deaf. Others suffered para-natal diseases—but that is another story:

A Deaf-Blind Athlete. There was this guy, I forgot his name. Age sixteen, mature-muscled, smart; a natural athlete. But he could neither see nor hear. We, the staff, communicated with him by finger-writing on the palm of his hand.

He was an excellent swimmer.

At the lake one day he climbed down the ladder and as was his habit, he lowered himself carefully into the water. He then tucked his head, took a shallow dive and swam like crazy. But he misjudged the dimensions of the swimming area and had plowed under the rope. And with a powerful American crawl, he sped maybe a hundred yards out into the area where kids and counselors were boating and canoeing.

There was no way to call him back. Shouting would do no good. Hand signals, less.

I plunged in and splashed to the rescue. But he continued on frantically, further and further from us.

Finally he got it. He stopped, cocked his ears and waited. I reached him, tapped his shoulder, wrote "come" in his palm and led him back to the swimming area.

The other kids, splashing with excitement as their counselors narrated the chase, let loose a great cheer.

I have so far been writing mostly about the boys. But my favorite place to hang out was Blue Cabin. In an effort to provide children with a meaningful visual vocabulary, each cabin, organized by gender and age, was named for a color. Blue Cabin housed little girls aged approximately five through seven. I enjoyed hanging out there. They loved games, songs and stories, the sillier the better.

And: They giggled whenever I showed up.

We composed a cheer:

I am me! You are you!
We're the girls of Cabin Blue!

Some years later I landed a job at Goddard College. I was its first graduate dean.

I yelled for quiet in the dining hall so that I could make an announcement... probably "Quiet Everybody: Shut Up!"

From the back of the hall came a shout:

"I hear the voice of Bobby Belenky!"

It was one of the Blue Cabin girls, now a college student.

Years later, another Blue Cabin girl became a professor of social work at a fine women's college. I met her in New York where she first worked; then later at the school.

There were others.

But many campers never did attain success in the eyes of the world. Some suffered additional major handicaps including retardation, brain damage or psychosis. Some had families that overprotected them to the extent that their social skills attenuated. Others remained forever timid and withdrawn, inexperienced in negotiating the world outside of their homes.

And many came from economically disadvantaged homes often in racially segregated communities.

I thought we had done well by viewing all kids equally as benign mischief-makers, spirited, fun-loving and with considerable hope of dealing with a difficult and often unfair world.

A research idea: The U.S. in those days was suffering from an epidemic of social class related blindness caused by a surfeit of oxygen given to premature babies in modern hospitals.

Hospitals in affluent communities were able to afford the expensive new leak-proof incubators that by default administered high levels of the gas to the developing infant. These in turn caused constriction of nascent retina arterioles that could no longer contain the flood of the newly generated blood flow. The arterioles then ruptured causing damage to the retina. Thus blindness.

What this led to was a disproportionate increase in visual disability among the children of the rich, usually full blindness.

At Camp Marcella it meant that income and race had unusual effects—more rich white kids were handicapped than were poor black kids. Camp Marcella blacks, unique in American culture, were the favored group at least along the dimension of that one measure of health. Total blindness was disproportionately present among the affluent white kids.

What did that mean in terms of social perception? Which group was now normative? How was racism now expressed? Did race remain a factor in perceptions of competence?

White kids needed help. Black kids were blessed with independence.

Well... I was not yet a student of psychology and such matters remained as part of a sea of invisible correlates in which I was unknowingly immersed then and well into extreme geezerdom.

***

In any event, I graduated from college with many interests, latent and otherwise, and a modicum of competence.

Next came autumn and an interim of indecision as above mentioned: Enrollment at the Columbia University School of Business, a few weeks as a copy boy, and leaving the three summers at The New Jersey Camp for Blind Children behind. What to do now?

It was obvious that I had come to a dead end.

I sought the advice of Ms Josephine L. Taylor, then Education Commissioner of the New Jersey Commission for the Blind, my ultimate boss. Camp Marcella was under her aegis.

"Jo," I said. "I have no idea what to do in the world. I must find a way to make a living. A career. What do you advise?"

Without hesitation, she proclaimed:

"You should become a psychologist for blind children!" "Of course!" I said. "That is just exactly what I shall do!"

So, I headed at once to Teachers College, Columbia University, to enroll in their Clinical Psychology, Ph.D. program.

Unfortunately ... I had not previously taken more than a review course in psychology and was thus totally ignorant and unprepared to pass the required Graduate Record Exam in that field.

Okay: I shall catch up!

Retaining my bursar's card from the School of Business, I spent long hours and many dreary days in the college library perusing elementary psychology textbooks and all sorts of primary psych material, some of it actually fascinating.

When next administered, I took the Graduate Record Exam, passed it with an okay score. And celebrated.

Then, I applied to the Columbia University doctoral program in Clinical Psychology, was accepted ... and Hooray!

Academia Redux

Graduate education was good. In some ways better than that: Stimulating for the most part; well beyond tolerable. Classes were mostly held as tiny seminars where discussions were often lively and absorbing.

Turned out that I knew a little more than I thought I knew. One day, for example, we discussed schizophrenia. Well, although I read a bit about it, I actually was on shaky ground. Nonetheless I spouted off, mumbling about the isolation from family and friends because of an incapacity to perceive the needs of others and to act accordingly.

One of my classmates commented: "So, Bob, it seems that you are a Sullivanian!"

In fact, although I had dimly heard of the seminal psychiatrist, Harry Stack Sullivan, I had not yet read any of his work and, except for hearsay, knew precious little about him.

"Yeh," I stammered.

Teachers College, Columbia, has long been a fount of progressive education. The points of view it promotes are akin to established wisdom in the progressive schools I attended, both elementary and secondary. So ... I fit right in.

Community Committees

Now back to the present, friends, and a few words about the impending nomination of Kendal Retirement Community residents to our Residents' Council. What I am about to say does not derive from deliberations of the Nominations Committee. Rather, these are my own thoughts.

First: How shall we find names to offer the Nominations Committee?

We must first consider the purpose of the Residents' Council.

May I suggest that it is to provide a framework for the Kendal community to function smoothly, efficiently and effectively?

Smoothly, efficiently and effectively; yes, of course. But to what end?

The end is our pending departure from this world.

We each have this happy downward slope waiting in our near future.

Kendal, you see, is in fact our purgatory where we bid farewell to family, friends, art, politics, the very earth and sky; indeed to all and everything, palpable or imagined.

The agenda of advanced age is to meditate on what we were and may in part still be. It is neither to regret nor to celebrate; and never to deny but thoughtfully to revisit that which remains alive or in fantasy.

It is therefore the task of the Kendal community via the Residents' Council to make way for all of it, and to facilitate its transformation into art, poetry, music, literature and dreams.

And, while searching for names to submit to the Nominations Committee for council membership, we may well be advised to consider both fellow residents who show an organizational bent but also to recognize others—the fantasists, the musicians, artists, poets, among us as well as those whose autumn frailties are all too soon evident.

As a community we have become expert in the arts and crafts of shared witness and support.

Let us therefore raise our banner and celebrate each and all the members of our panoply of selves.

Practice

Emerging from graduate school relatively unscathed—and financially unburdened as well—thanks to a generous US Public Health Service fellowship—I stepped into the world.

My first professional job was once again with the New Jersey Commission for the Blind. This time, my task was to conduct a survey of all the blind children in the state who in addition to suffering a vision loss were mentally retarded or psychotic.

I travelled throughout New Jersey, lists of handicapped children in hand. I was to track down each such whether at home or in an institution.

The goal was to determine if child and family were receiving adequate services from "The Commission."

I met with child, parents and/or caretakers, took notes, subsequently reporting my findings to boss, Josephine Taylor, at Commission headquarters in Newark.

What I learned: Most children were living at home and attending public school while receiving a variety of supplementary educational services, skilled and sympathetic special teachers and sophisticated curriculum materials geared to the needs and limitations of the sightless—all from the Commission for the Blind. In keeping with that state's progressive reputation, there was blessedly no institution for the blind in New Jersey

On the other hand a disturbing number of leftover children were relegated to wandering the halls of ancient, vast, neglectful and punitive state institutions for the retarded or the disturbed.

With master list in hand, I dutifully visited each New Jersey multiply-handicapped blind child no matter where residing, as well as parents, institutions for the retarded or the insane; teachers, and caretakers. And I entered the bowels of every institution for the retarded or co-handicapped. I also visited many public schools and spoke with countless teachers and parents.

I took prodigious notes and fell to sleep each night shaken and exhausted. The next day I would submit a report to the Commission, often in the person of Josephine Taylor herself.

The job was far from my expectation of the sanitized work of a clinical child psychologist but the sense that I was participating in an endeavor to improve the lives of society's most desperate and needy rewarded me with an earnest, almost religious, sense of gratification. Although a dedicated atheist, the work felt Holy.

A product of a Private School Education, I found myself immersed in the Real World.

There was this father, a sensitive, well educated man. He and his family lived by the sea. His daughter, five or six at the time, was sightless, had no speech and was given to perpetual, furious, animal-like howls and sobs.

"How might the New Jersey Commission for the Blind be of assistance to your daughter," I asked? "And to your wife and yourself," I added.

"Get me a rowboat," he answered in a low voice. "I will place our daughter in it. I will row her a mile or two out to sea ... and leave her there."

Playroom 81

An email just arrived from an old friend and new colleague.

I replied:

Hey, Charles (Or Chucky or Dr. Searcy or whatever you go by these days)!

I am SO happy to have received your email!

My GOD! You must be sixty-five! years old now. I remember you at the age of eight.

Our recent brief email exchange was a pleasant surprise, a delight; it got to me—not only because Playroom 81 and all of the people contacted with it—notably the Searcy family—were such important factors in my personal and professional development but because the entire experience was interesting on so many levels.

It was also great fun, for, I suspect, all of us. It may also have been helpful ... to the larger community.

You went through that entire period as a kid. Amazing.

And then you emerged from a period of personal struggle that was tough but surely also a learning experience.

And now you are a colleague, a psychologist on the cusp of a doctorate.

Wow! I would love to learn about your journey, your perspective, your reflections, what you have processed and how and what you learned as well as the thinking that led to your involvement in mental health as a profession that deals with the ways in which one attempts to intervene in the lives of others.

You may not have been aware of this in the old days, but Jay ("Jonathan") Clark and I were part of an experimental program based in Harvard's Graduate School of Education. It was called "The Shadow Faculty.[4]" The belief—a bit over-the-top perhaps— was that the Boston Public Schools were in disaster mode; on the road to collapse. When that happens, we, the professors and students of Harvard, would take over the whole operation, handle it properly. And save everybody.

Nervy or what?

The coordinator of The Shadow Faculty was Don Oliver, an enormously energetic and creative social studies professor.

Jay was a student at the Harvard Graduate School of Education at the time and I was an adjunct faculty

---

[4] https://www.thecrimson.com/article/1966/6/16/ed-schools-shadow-faculty-thirty-re-searchers/?page=single

member there by virtue of being on loan from my then job as psychologist in the suburban Newton, Mass. school system.

Jay and I had worked together before and were happy to continue doing so.

For the first step in The Shadow Faculty's experiment, we decided to take on imaginary administrative roles in the not yet existing utopian school system. Mine was to be director of counseling and mental health programs. As such I was to design and staff a fanciful system equipped to handle the mixed-up, uncertain, delinquent or otherwise problematic kid.

My style was—and indeed still is—to learn on the job. I was eager to jump right into the urban world, create a mock-up version of what seemed to be needed; then harness it—in a trial run to be evaluated in action over time.

The first task was to find a typical Boston community in which to work. On the recommendation of an interested priest in the white community bordering black Roxbury, we chose the Mission Hill Housing Project because it was centrally located; and it presented many classic urban problems including poverty, school failure and formidable racial segregation: Almost everyone north of Parker Street was black; and almost everyone south, white.

We proceeded with the conviction that not much headway is likely to be made by child guidance dolled out entirely within a school building. Way more sensible, we reasoned, for purposes of mental health—whatever that may be—would be to engage the entire community including families, friends, neighbors, housing, schools, churches and businesses.

We might then be in a position to engage, nurture and amplify existing personal and cultural strengths.

Far-out? Or what?

Playroom 81 was the result. It became a community-designed and created resource, owned, administered and staffed by neighbors; an after-school activities program for all the little kids, white, brown and black, in that highly segregated public housing complex. We were gadflies.

The program took place in the basement of 81 Parker Street.

Hence the name: Playroom 81.

Your mother, Barbara Searcy, loved the idea and immediately became the project's leader. Jay and I hung around as consultants and friends rather than experts.

The whole thing was ultimately in your mom's hands and in those of her friends. It was staffed both by black and white parents working together.

The housing project administration tolerated the project, co-operated or left it alone. All three, I guess.

And the Harvard Graduate School of Education obtained a grant that provided our program with an adequate operating budget.

And the entire community joined in because the program promised positive things for little kids and everybody.

And in Playroom 81, Jay, Harvard and I imagined a model for the utopian school/community-based mental health program that we hoped would emerge.

We were all fortunate in your mom's leadership! She was strong-minded, sensible, fun, modest, respected and intelligent; a natural, quiet leader. It was her involvement that made the whole thing possible and popular.

Lots of other people were great as well, mothers, fathers, children and neighbors—black and white.

We soon came to realize that the Harvard consulting team consisting just of Jay and me, two white guys, needed to be supplemented by a black professional—from the community and with a position on the Shadow Faculty.

Jonathan Kozol, a mutual friend, suggested Jim Reed.

Jim was ten years or so older than we were then; an artist, a big guy, a commanding presence; committed to his vision as well as to black liberation; having suffered and underestimated because of racism, he was intimidating to some, impressive to all whether at Harvard or within the community.

We managed to work together, Jim, Jay and I, but the road was rocky; paved with lively conversations—many but not nearly enough—overlaying fundamental distrust. Jim often felt that Jay and I functioned out of unconscious white skin privilege. He may have been right; we tried to do better.

The next step: We brought in a few local teenagers as assistants to the parent/staff members. These were kids who functioned marginally in school; students who often had dealings with guidance counselors for academic and behavioral reasons. Or those who were invisible loners.

You may remember two of them: Gail and Arthur. I don't recall how we found them. Both were strong characters, quick-wit-ted but academically disengaged.

Initially some parents were horrified. The thought of having local teens—who themselves were in need of adult guidance— taking responsibility, albeit limited, for one's children, left them to say the least, skeptical. Yet after a brief try-out period, most of the teens, notably Gail and Arthur, did responsible work, became well liked and won the trust of parents.

Both became key members of the entire operation. Gail proved an efficient, smart presence almost equal to that of the mothers. Arthur, a shy fellow from the Black South, spoke with an accent that at first was hard for me to understand. But it soon became evident that he had a sharp, subtle wit especially appreciated by the children.

I imagined Arthur one day becoming a writer or monologue entertainer. I once shared that prediction with him; I could not tell how he received it. His face was expressionless.

As our own contribution to the program, Jay, Jim and I tried to enlarge the relevant experience of the neighborhood parents. As a program we took trips to Harvard for Shadow Faculty meetings, to New York City where we visited the Ford Foundation and even met with a black guy I knew who was a funding agent; then it was on to Washington for a national conference on poverty.

We also took trips to the beach and, with some of the older kids, to the woods of New Hampshire.

All this was in line with our conviction that although counseling the child in school—absent a broader context—may be a standard albeit limited model, more fundamental changes may be seen if the child—no matter the age—is involved on many levels in the lived community.

Playroom 81 was in fact the community's own program, not ours; neither was it that of some school principal or higher-up bureaucrat. Given the opportunity, local people revealed leadership skills that had not previously been visible, bureaucratically speaking. At least not to us.

And involvement in the world beyond the local community did indeed make sense, we felt; it was, we concluded, vital.

With a broad focus, everyone stands to benefit.

Take segregation. White parents from south of Parker Street participated fully in the program side by side with black parents from the north side. That made for a larger, less conflicted, more pleasant and more livable neighborhood.

Regardless of color, parents from both sub-communities planned together, worked together, and socialized together with little or no overt evidence of racial animus.

Utopia or what?

Big shots visited Playroom 81. Ted Kennedy was one; and a group of Soviet educators spent an afternoon with us. And from time to time various professors wandered through.

But our experiment never became flush with publicity nor with academic prominence. This was probably because the Boston School System never did collapse as predicted thus, unfortunately, we never had a chance to take over.

But Playroom 81 did have a significant influence on the lives of everyone who participated—many local children, teenagers, parents; indeed on the entire community.

And the remainder of my professional career contained elements of the experience.

* * *

Oh, do you remember when we took you and some other kids to a New Hampshire state park and we all sat around a camp-fire for hours talking about nothing in particular? We did that several times.

We all went to the beach, too.

That kind of experience got me thinking that perhaps the best way to work with people is to lift them—with friends—out of their customary scene for a while to immerse them in a safe but unfamiliar setting where a dramatic perspective on everything customary becomes possible.

Well ... that about sums up my view of counseling.

And that is also what brought Mary, me, our kids, Alice and Michael ... and our then dog, Melanie, to Vermont in 1970.

Chuck: I was wondering . . . how about let's get together and reminisce about these things? Mary and I now live in a very nice retirement community and don't travel much because of extreme old age. But, if you and your wife would like a vaca–tion in lovely New Hampshire, we would be delighted to put you up.

The invitation holds for any and all members of the Searcy Clan.

Also ... you and I might communicate electronically. And continue to share thoughts ....

My love to you, your mom—if she is still in this world—and to your brothers and sisters and to everybody's grandchildren.

Bob

* * *

Jay Clark Comments—July 12, 2019

Bob: You've captured so many of the wacky, informative and compelling experiences that you and I encountered as we entered the worlds on both sides of Parker St.

I think of that course we taught about young children at one end of the basement while the mothers ran a play group for three-year-olds at the other end.

When people raised questions about the behavior of young kids we would migrate to the other end where the kids themselves were more than happy to act out in ways that stimulated our discussions.

Or that time when, on the spur of the moment, we rented a school bus to drive out to some nearby park in the middle of a snow storm, and everybody, kids and adults, ran madly about slipping and sliding and throwing snowballs at each other and having the time of their lives.

Or, the time Jim dressed up as Santa and scared the living daylights out of (some) of the kids about the imminent possibility of Santa visiting those children who continued to misbehave, whether at the playground or at home!

Or in DC rushing around to grocery stores in search of a head of lettuce for Dodie, one of the mothers.

Or Barbara Searcy dropping to a whisper in the face of Edward McCormac's shout: The Mothers of Which??!! in compensation for the fact that the Speaker of The House of the United States House was Stone Deaf!

You did right in letting things roll and roll they did in a manner quite unrivaled in the course of my professional life which has tended in the direction of the wild and (relatively) unexpected.

I'm immensely grateful to you for including me in your venture; the two years we spent, first imagining and then setting in motion the series of events that led to: Playroom 81.

It sounds as if Chuck had to struggle with major ups and downs on his way to becoming a psychologist. I imagine that Barbara Searcy, his mother, was a huge influence upon his ability to survive that long trip.

I Do Swear ...

... that each day from now until I have written the final word of this memoir, I shall dutifully recall and record at least one memory.

... the very least that I can do.

Maybe a book will be the result. Maybe even a good one.

Who is to say?

Community Mental Health

The Crimson Raiders (a fake name) was a notorious motorcycle gang headquartered on the edge of the city not far from my work … I can't remember exactly where.

I had taken a job as a community psychologist. I was based at a formidable mental health center but my work obliged me to wander various neighborhoods which I did each day in eager anticipation.

Interesting characters. There was this gigolo guy. I shall call him "Albert" for the purpose of this essay. He was a garrulous, engaging fellow, a natural host; a charmer; a professional seducer. Slick. He made his living as a gigolo which, the kids explained, is an "escort," essentially a male prostitute. A rich women who needed a date would call for an appointment. And off they would go, out together for the evening.

His "office" was the phone in his otherwise spare apartment.

Albert hired a teenage neighborhood girl as his secretary. She answered the phone in a well-modulated voice and kept his appointments in order.

The girl introduced me to Albert.

Albert, kids and grownups in turn dropped the name "Crimson Raiders" from time to time. "They run this neighborhood," I was told.

I wanted to be introduced.

I asked a couple of teenagers to take me to the gang's head-quarters, an undistinguished clapboard building. I knocked timidly on the door. An unsmiling young man wearing a single earring let us in.

The Crimson Raiders. Their leader, now long dead, was a hardy fellow of Irish descent. Gracious. Pot-bellied, paternal in a gruff but engaging manner. He referred to the gang members as "my boys."

I shall call him "Mac" for the purposes of this reporting which I have endeavored to offer true to the events related, redacting only identifying data.

Mac was old by the standards of his profession. Thirty-eight; exactly my age. He wore a scruffy beard that was beginning to turn grey.

He introduced himself with a convivial smile and he spoke with a ringing tough-guy street intonation.

I reached for his right hand to shake as convention dictates. Three fingers were missing, the third, fourth and fifth from the thumb.

"A gun fight," he explained. "Years ago."

"It is it is glorious thing to be a pirate king!"[5] I sang under my breath.

Through this and later conversations I came to understand that The Crimson Raiders was both a motorcycle club and a business. The latter consisted of importing drugs from Mexico and wholesaling them on the streets of the city.

"And what is your own work?" he asked.

"I am a Community Mental Health Psychologist," I said. "I focus on children, youth and families and on supporting what may be healthy in the community."

"Interesting," he said. "My brother is a youth consultant to the mayor. I would love to do something like that myself."

"No kidding! But," I wondered, "what about the drugs that you and your boys bring in?"

"We do only wholesale," Mac explained. "If I learn that somebody who buys drugs from us retails them to kids, I send my boys out to teach him a lesson."

"How?"

"We beat the crap out of him. Look," he continued, "we want to help kids just like you do. Kids look up to us. We have a lot of influence. We appreciate that."

"Interesting," I said.

---

[5]https://www.youtube.com/watch?v=jQ7SVMVrick

"You know," Mac repeated. "I would love to advise the mayor just like my brother does."

"Here's an idea," I said. "How about we train your boys in child psychology? We could teach them how to play a positive role for kids in the neighborhood.

"Maybe," I continued, "we could recruit the University Extension Service—the adult education department—to sponsor such a course. Then if any of your boys decides to go back to school, they could begin with a leg up and a few academic credits."

"Terrific!" he said. "Let's give it a try."

I headed to the offices of the Extension Service and proposed the course as well as reasons for it. I then put the idea in writing as requested and submitted it. Some days later, I received a letter of acceptance including tuition waivers. I hurried at once to the gang headquarters to show it to Mac who was delighted.

I suggested that our first session be held in a meeting room at the hospital where I worked. Mac said that would be terrific.

Reserving the room was no problem.

One week later a swarm of Crimson Raiders roared up to the hospital, parked their bikes and marched in the front door.

Oh, what a sight they were! —Red bandannas and helmets, long hair, leather jackets, earrings, tattoos, chains, boots, beards and scowling faces. The whole thing.

Doctors in suits and ties, prim secretaries, bespectacled, white-coated white doctors with well-combed grey hair, men and women clutching clipboards—all of these stared judgmentally at my students who for their part carried themselves erect and with a sense of propriety—and not a few sly glances in my direction.

My students slumped themselves at the desks provided and the class was in session.

A fellow raised his hand.

"Yes?" I asked.

"Why are you doing this, Doc?"

"Mac and I thought it might be good for you," I replied.

"But don't you know that when you deal with us, you are dealing with organized crime?"

"If so," I said, "this course might open new options for you." The guy peered at me, eyebrow raised skeptically. "And why are you here?" I countered. "Mac made us come," he replied.

In any event, the course thus begun continued for at least a half dozen sessions; no longer at the hospital but rather on the second floor of a Catholic church rectory opposite the local middle school. In addition to the motorcycle gang members, a few neighborhood teenagers joined us, eager, they explained, "to make a positive difference in a child's life."

The fellow I remember best was Johnny James, a great kid. Long since dead. Smart. But extreme; on the crazy side. He showed up, he said, because he liked to hang around motorcycle guys. I imagined that he also got hooked because we talked about personal stuff, how each of us grew up. That sort of thing pretty much dominated the discussions.

Johnny was nuanced, bright, articulate, respected by others; eventually perhaps a leader although at this moment driven more by inner passions that were as yet neither framed nor tamed.

One day the neighborhood kids got word that a group of Boston College undergraduates planned to throw a party for them in the basement of the Catholic church mentioned above.

Johnny was all for it.

The local priest helped with arrangements.

I had many colleagues in Boston College at the time and got word from a couple of them on how it went.

"Catastrophically."

A student's purse was stolen, several neighborhood boys propositioned BC girls, and a BC boy got punched in the face. The delegation left in tears.

"Johnny!" I scolded when next I saw him. "That's awful! Those students wanted to help you make this a better neighborhood and you behaved like crazy people! The students' feelings were hurt and now they think you are a bunch of ungrateful thugs.

"What were you kids thinking?"

"Whoa!" he said. "Those rich kids came down here to help us, the 'underprivileged,' but they don't know us. They have no idea who we are or what we need. They think we're dumb and that they are the smart ones. But the girl left her pocket book on the chair when she went off to dance with Mickey and then one of their guys tried to make out with Gloria who is Jimmy's girlfriend.

"They can't act like that without getting hurt. They don't understand that this is a dangerous community and we are a rough bunch that need to be respected. So we just needed to teach them to respect our delinquency. We did it for their sakes.

"How else were we going to teach them?"

Race

"Mac," I said. "I can't help but notice that everyone in your club is white."

"True," he replied. "But that's just how it happens to be. We are actually not a racist club. When Martin Luther King came to town, we drove our bikes alongside to protect him."

Chivalry

One day around lunchtime I came to Mac's apartment to ask him something about the course. A couple of guys were lounging around the kitchen. "Where's Mac?" I asked. "There," they said, pointing to the bedroom.

The door stood ajar. I knocked.

"Come in!"

Mac was sprawled in the double bed with his arms around two stark-naked young women partially submerged under the sheets.

"I am protecting them from my boys," Mac explained.

Ignorance

One day I dropped in to discuss something with Mac. The boys were across the room cracking up about some exploit. I could hear most of what they were saying. It had to do with violence; probably rape.

"Please, boys," I said. "Do not discuss those things when I am around. I don't want to know."

"Yeh. Okay," they said.

Party!

Some weeks later, Mary (my wife), and I were invited to a party in the neighborhood. It was to be held in an abandoned house that the kids around Albert, the gigolo, took over.

Lots of kids were there, maybe thirty to fifty, all of them in a great mood. The electricity had long since been turned off in the building, but music was blaring from a huge, battery-operated tape player, and the room was lit by flickering kerosene lanterns.

Everybody was dancing, rapidly, wildly, flaying about, not quite to the music. I spotted Albert and we greeted each other, but I didn't see any of the Crimson Raiders or Mac or any of his lieutenants. Beer was consumed. I'm not sure what else. Cigarette and pot smoke hung heavy in the air.

A kid walked up, a smirk on his face. "Hey, hi-ya doin', Doc?"

"Great," I said. "Nice party."

"Yeh. Everybody's here."

"By the way, Doc," he continued, "how did you get here? I mean, hey, ain't no trains or busses. No nothing."

"I came by car," I explained. "Brought my wife. She's over there. I'll introduce you in a minute."

"But where did you park your car? There are a lot of car thieves in this neighborhood, you know."

"I'm not worried," I said. "All the car thieves are right here at the party."

"But, Doc, don't you think you ought to go out and check?" he persisted.

"No need to," I said. "I'm not worried."

He shrugged and wandered off. Another kid, a girl, approached, smiling.

"Hi, Doc," she said barely repressing a grin. "I hear you came by car. Wow, that was so brave! Aren't you afraid that it could be gone when you're ready to go home? Somebody might jump the wires and drive off with it."

"That won't happen," I said. "The car is a three-cylinder SAAB. Very unusual. Nobody in this neighborhood knows how to jump-start those things."

"You'd better check on it anyway," she said. "One never knows," she added in a tone of maternal care.

"Nope, not necessary," I said. "Not at all. Besides, I'm happy standing right here."

I was soon surrounded by a half dozen more kids, all in bubbly moods, laughingly showing concern for my car.

"Okay," I said at last. "You win. I'm going now and I will check on the car. Here I go."

A throng of giggling teenagers grabbed my hands, shoved me from behind, pulled me from the front, opened the door to let me through while others surrounded Mary and similarly accompanied her to the street.

A moment later we were on the sidewalk just where I had parked my car.

"Okay, kids," I said with as civil a voice as I could muster. "Where is it?"

On hearing the question, they proceeded to laugh it up with joyous abandonment as they grabbed my hands and Mary's and led us down the street to a dark alley where my precious black, sun-roofed, old-fashioned, three-cylinder SAAB coupe lay, its nose no more than two feet from one wall and it's rear the same distance from the opposite one. It was an impressive achievement.

Getting at once into the spirit, I joined the laughter. "How did you manage this?" I asked. Understandably. They answered all at once, a jumble of words and giggles. But the meaning was clear. As I had predicted, none of them could figure out how to jump the ignition wires of the SAAB. So they did the next best thing. A bunch of kids—boys and girls as well—worked in concert to lift the vehicle. They then carried it a block and a half to deposit it neatly between the two walls of the alley.

"Brilliant!" I said.

With that and working together once again they managed to raise the car; then rotated it forty-five degrees so that its nose faced the alley's exit.

"We can leave it parked here until it's time to go home," I suggested.

And so we returned together to the party. Cracking jokes all the way.

Vermont

One day I bade farewell to The Neighborhood. I had accepted a job at Goddard College in Vermont.

Mary, the kids, Melanie—our then dog—and I packed our car, drove to Vermont and settled in an old farmhouse on a remote dirt road.

One evening, Mary's elderly mother was visiting us from her home in Ann Arbor. We sat by the fireplace, chatting. The kids were in school. A wood fire caressed us.

We heard a distant roar, first barely perceptible then building to a disturbing intensity. Motorcycles!

The gang had arrived. Heavy boots crashed on our porch. The front door swung open and an army of leather jacketed, helmeted, pistol-carrying, kerchief-wearing, long-haired, rude and ruddy fellows invaded our paradise.

"We came to see you," one of them announced, "because we were having an argument. You are our gang shrink. We want you to help us settle it!"

"Sure," I said. "Take a seat, guys. I'll give it a try."

We spent the next hour, maybe less, hearing first one side, and then the other, each stated with passion and accusations. But there was no violence.

I've forgotten the substance. It's been a long time. But soon the matter was settled to everyone's satisfaction.

The men stood, headed for the kitchen, helped themselves to bread, chicken, cake and apple cider—we had neither beer nor liquor—until they cleaned the place out. Then they arose, tramped out the front door mumbling "thank-you."

Then they mounted the bikes and roared off into the night.

"Never again speak to me again of the peace and quiet of country life," Mary's mother said.

Woof

Woof!

Woof, Milly says again, slyly swooshing her swishy tail.

Woof woof arf arf arf woof.

That's silly, Milly, I say. And I don't believe a word of it.

Grrrr! Milly growls.

You are joking, I say.

Yip! Yip! Yip! Yip! laughs Milly.

You think you are so clever, I say.

Yipyipyipyip! Milly cracks up.

Enough, I say. It's time now for your afternoon walk.

YIP YIP YIP YIP! shouts Milly at the top of her voice.

We drive across town to the park.

In the car, Milly sits on the back seat and peers out the window.

As we approach, she wags her tail while wiggling her entire hindquarters.

We get out of the car.

I put her little red ball in the cup at the end of the pink stick.

And I give the ball a super fling.

Milly dances after it, wildly swishing her tail.

She chomps the ball in her mouth, brings it to me ... And drops it at my feet.

"Fling it again!" she says with her tail.

I fling it once again. She snarfs it up and returns it. I fling it yet again. And again. And again,

My arm is tired. "That's it, Milly!" I say. "Time to go." Milly hangs her head. She is sad.

I open the car door and toss a bacon-flavored dog treat onto the back seat.

Milly jumps in, stretches out and chomps on the treat-on-the-seat while mumbling,

"Thank you, Daddy!"

. . . with evident sincerity.

Elijah

Passover is a venerable holiday yet one that is contemporary. Its holy meal, the Seder, celebrates the pariah, the homeless, the stateless, the immigrant, the despised and the persecuted. It offers the eternal possibility that the vagrant visitor may in fact be God's emissary.

In a traditional Seder, guests leave their shoes at the door when they arrive and they relax, get comfortable, and eat. Shoes remain symbolic affirmations that they are at home. The door is left ajar and a cup of wine is set aside should a homeless stranger happen by. Who is to say? The unkempt wanderer may prove to be an Archangel, perhaps the Prophet Elijah.

The Seder is a feast of inclusion that embraces the family writ large. We, the fortunate, are at the table but so are our cousins, those who are oppressed and homeless; the tortured, the tormented, the imprisoned and the refugee. Together we envision the perfect home we have so longed for whether it be in Jerusalem, New York, or The Emerald City. How better to address America's current crisis at its southern border?

The Poop

Despite recent witticisms, half-witticisms and utter disbelief, some Kendal residents (Milly and me) are persuaded that we really could use a better approach here with respect to the collection of dog feces, one that is more comprehensive, less mechanical and absent interpersonal (or doggerel) accusation. From recent discussions, it appears that Kendal's concern is both the poop itself as well as antediluvian animal/owner behavior including aggression, running away and use of the leash.

What if Kendal were to require a small advance "deposit" for each dog's deposit? Perhaps, say, twenty-five dollars. The money would go into a fund for hiring an animal behaviorist who would convene quarterly group consultation sessions—attendance: Strongly recommended. There, dog/owner interactions would be observed, critiqued and better approaches practiced. Problems—dog poop as but one example—would be discussed and solutions arrived at together by all present.

This is but one example of the sort of group-based, non-authoritarian, humane rather than mechanistic, potentially amusing approaches that would at once earn my full support as well as that of Milly, my canine companion.

Respectfully submitted,

Appropriation

After a half century, the following still gets to me ....

My supervisor calls me into his office. "Do you think it is appropriate for a representative of our celebrated mental hospital to appear in court at two in the morning in the company of a young delinquent?"

"Yes," I said. "I do."

An odd interchange it surely was for a number of reasons not the least of which is that I never, under any circumstances, found myself in court at such an ungodly hour and surely not for the reason alleged. I need my sleep.

Okay. I confess. I do have certain problems with some people in authority. But only with the mindless sort. Sadly, the world has more than its share ...

An example: When employed by a certain local institution of higher learning, a colleague told me that its president had received a call from a board member who warned, "As long as you keep that asshole Belenky on your faculty, you're not getting another penny from me!"

What could I possibly have done to spark such an outburst?

Answer: The probable cause was a newspaper report of my appearance before a State Senate Investigating Committee. I was quoted as having offered uncharitable opinions about certain disciplinary practices in Boston's schools. These mostly consisted of delivering a hard whack with a piece of bamboo rattan on the knuckles of the offending child often drawing blood and always causing pain. I had publicly called the practice "savage."

Now, here is where my reputation was made:

I had accepted a weekly one day consultantship with a Reform School for Girls, an institution known for its modern practices. I was to help create a counseling service. It soon appeared that I myself was to be the entire service.

I arrived on a sparkling autumn day. The sky was blue. The campus, pristine. There were flowers, trees and bushes everywhere. Amid walkways and tasteful, nineteenth century brick buildings, girls in trim brown uniforms strolled. The impression was not unlike that of a prep school or college campus.

The headmistress had been a respected prison reform advocate earlier in her career. She greeted me cordially and offered a cup of tea served politely by a uniformed adolescent inmate.

"We are so very pleased that you are on board," the head-mistress said. I replied that I in turn was looking forward to helping her and the children as best I could.

She suggested that group counseling might be an advisable approach because it would enable me to reach the maximum number of kids during each week's visit. I was, it appeared, to be the only member of the mental health staff. The institution held some two hundred fifty residents, as I recall, most of whom might sorely be in need of counseling services.

"If you are willing," she said, "we will assign a staff member to assist you. In that way you could serve a training as well as a direct service function."

"Yes, of course," I answered. "An excellent idea."

When I showed up the following week, I was directed to my assigned meeting room. A large, middle aged woman sat glumly at the center surrounded by chairs.

"I am your assistant," she said.

Girls of various ages filed in and took seats while nodding without expression in my direction.

I introduced myself. I explained that this was where a very special meeting would be held each week and where, hopefully, people would support one another and feel free to speak their minds without fear of punishment.

"What is said in this room, stays in this room," I said. "It is not to be shared with anyone on campus. Agreed?"

"Agreed," came the answer from the group.

The discussion got off to a slow start. Gradually there were questions; then complaints, jokes, expressions of anger and sadness, as well as miscellaneous gripes plus a few confessions of minor misdeeds. It all went by quickly and was difficult to keep in my head but I did my best.

An older, soft-spoken teenager told of a recent gang fight during which a girl was stripped, then raped with a broom stick.

A little girl, eleven years old, angrily related yet another incident. I cannot remember the story. But I do recall her tearful fury.

My assistant sat, stolid and voiceless. The girls seemed to ignore her.

I returned a week later. Group members followed by my assistant filed into our room and took their seats.

The angry eleven year old was not among them.

"Where is she?" I asked.

"Being punished," my assistant explained.

"How? Where?

"She's in solitary," one of the girls said.

"Solitary? For what?"

"For what she said last week in our meeting, I guess," a girl replied.

"But," I said looking at my assistant, "I had clearly explained that what is said in our group is to remain in the group."

My assistant, blank-faced, said nothing.

"How long has she been in solitary?"

"Since after last week's meeting," a girl said.

After the session I found my way to the isolation room. The the door was unlocked; slightly ajar. I entered. The light was dim. The room was bare. The angry girl sat on the floor. A pair of knitting needles was in her hands.

"I am going to kill myself with these," she mumbled, absently poking the needles toward her stomach.

We sat together for some minutes. At my request, she absently handed me her needles. But I never learned her story.

Lunchtime. The Director chatted with the staff. Food was served by, silent, unsmiling, uniformed young prisoners.

I sat next to a woman who seemed, like myself, to be an outsider. She introduced herself as an investigator from the Massachusetts State Senate. Her task was to look into conditions in public custodial institutions for children.

"Wow!" I said. "I can help you."

Right after lunch I took her to the isolation room where she interviewed the unhappy little girl. I was elsewhere.

Afterward, the investigator thanked me, moved and ashen-faced. And off she went to interview others including the institution's director.

Well, I had obviously come to the end of my consultantship and was certain to be fired. Rather than wait, I thought it best to take the initiative and simply quit, hopefully in a way that would do some good.

On returning home, I called all of Boston's news sources, TV, radio and print.

A day or so later, our living room was filled with journalists, TV cameras, microphones and wires. The story went out.

I was far from the only person who spoke out on how juveniles were treated in Massachusetts. Several other experienced professionals did so as well. As a result, all state reform schools were soon closed.

It was hoped that the financial savings would be invested in community-based programs. But that was not to be. The monies were instead dumped into the state's general fund.

And I became a confirmed trouble maker at a certain fine local institution of higher learning.

Promised tenure was denied. Fine. I was ready to hang it up anyway.

But a distinguished law school professor I did not know personally called to explain that proper academic procedure had not been followed in my case. He arranged for us to meet with the College's president.

Pro Bono.

A violation of contract issue!

I had been hired as faculty member without tenure. The tenure decision was to have been made by the faculty at a duly convened meeting after three years. Three years passed but no meeting was held.

"A clear violation of college by-laws," the professor explained.

"But," said the president who exuded the charm of an experienced political appointee, "that is the procedure we have followed since our founding in 1849."

"You should not say that," the law professor advised, "or this institution will find itself liable for breach of contract suits going back to 1849."

The president then said, "Hurrumph," and graciously offered to pay me a full year's salary—$15,000—if I would just shut up and get lost.

I shook his hand and accepted the deal wisely refraining from kissing him on both cheeks.

The following year was delicious. I accepted a half-time job at Boston University and a second halftime stint at the Massachusetts Mental Health Center.

Yet I remained restless. And so at the end of the year, Mary, the kids, Melanie (our faithful dog) and I moved to Vermont where we went on to live happy and productive lives. All of this thanks to the kind gift from my previous employer.

"Goddard," my Boston University dean said when I came to bid him farewell, "is the perfect place for a guy like you."

Mary went on to do significant work in women's studies and I helped design and implement Goddard College's Graduate Studies Program. And Alice and Michael, by then pre-teens, were more than delighted to enter free, new lives in Vermont's untamed wilderness.

Goddard

Goddard then was at the apex of its counterculture incarnation. Lifestyle experimentation of every louche and imaginable sort was on the agenda and with any person, being or substance. I recognized at once that, although not a practiced educational experimenter or actual hippy, my cranky, counter-culture roots had found nurturing soil at last.

Goddard had an admirable history, a solid connection to the local Vermont community, and a commitment to reaching for the very essence of the learning experience, not merely the form. Most impressive was its "Adult Degree Program"— or "ADP"—in which each student designed his or her own course of study and criteria for ultimate evaluation. Students met for a couple of weeks each year, planned their work, and mulled over preliminary thoughts. There was a second meeting six months later for the presentation of interim study results; finally a session a half year beyond that in which the work was presented for approval to faculty and fellow students.

All the while, students would remain in touch with each other by mail and phone as well as with professors who were actually consultants more than instructors.

It was a utopian model, idealistic certainly, but for many—if not most—adults it was practical, compatible, stimulating and effective.

Our own planned program, the "GGP"—The Goddard Graduate Program—was to be an elaboration of the ADP model. One difference was that, in addition to the three annual meetings on the Goddard campus, frequent gatherings would be held locally in public libraries, schools or students' homes.

It was also unique in that beside the Goddard-based faculty member, our program sought out and employed a part time consultant accessible to the student, who was expert in the that student's particular area of study. We called such a person the "Field Faculty" member.

Those of us located at Goddard—known as "Core Faculty"— while often not conversant with the details or even particular area of each student's interest, consulted with him or her on the study's design and helped to find appropriate resources. We endeavored to locate and approve the Field Faculty member and to bring together a committee—Core and Field Faculty—to assess the student's final study and portfolio.

The design worked well with very few hitches and brought us many compliments. It was in fact similar to the process used in European graduate studies; indeed world wide at a doctoral level.

Soon after I was hired to be both dean and Core Faculty member, I found a second second person to join me. This was Ed Bottome, a popular history professor at Boston University who was about to lose his job because of his left wing politics and association with the famous and even more popular B.U. historian, Howard Zinn. Students closed B.U. down for over a week when it was announced that Ed was to be fired.

We were delighted to welcome Ed into our ranks. And Zinn remained a friend of the program.

Ed and I came from very different backgrounds. He had been a military man in post-WWII Europe. "You can't trust anybody but a turncoat," he liked to say. The reason: The turncoat has intimate knowledge of the enemy's intimate reality whereas the liberal possesses only ideology, book learning and sentiment. Ed had been present when high ranking officers bandied about end-of-the-world nuclear war strategy and tactics, an experience that left an unforgettable searing impression on him. He wrote a good book on the subject, "Balance of Terror," Beacon Press,1986.

Ed and I did a lot of talking about the kind of graduate program we wanted to develop. We agreed that we aimed for something that would lead to this becoming a more thoughtful, humane, and better world.

Students

Once we agreed on a basic design for our program, our next task was to recruit students. We did the expected. We let our former colleagues in the academic world know. We advertised. And we spread the word to business, social and political institutions that might have in interest in what we were offering.

The most promising of these was an organization of civil service union leaders in New York City. One of its members, Alan Gartner, now deceased, was an old friend of Mary's, my wife, and a colleague of mine in the Newton, Massachusetts Public Schools.

As a result, our first student group—numbering perhaps thirty—was composed largely of very smart, no-nonsense Black and Hispanic union leaders, both male and female, as well as a smattering of people of both sexes wishing to further their careers or stimulate their creativity. We were to meet together for one full week to initiate the program.

We assembled the group in one of Goddard's classrooms.

As dean, I rose up to welcome all present.

At once, a hand was raised.

"Yes," I said.

"We wish to inform the faculty and fellow students," a middle aged black man announced, "that the Third World Collective of the Goddard College Graduate Program met this morning. It was agreed that you and Ed Bottome are to be

relieved of your duties at once and that we will henceforth take charge of the program."

"Whoa!" I said. "Hold on there ..."

Ed pulled at my shirttail. "Sit down, Bob," he whispered. "Let's see how this develops."

"Okay," I said turning to the group. "How does the Third World Collective propose that we proceed?"

"We shall convene separate from yourselves," the man said, "for as long as needed. When we are finished, we will meet again in plenary session to inform you of the results and the plan for what is to follow."

"Wow!" I responded. "Well, if it's gotta be, it's gotta be. Go ahead, Third World Students, do your thing. Just don't forget to call us when you're finished."

With that, the meeting adjourned.

Ed and I, the white students and Goddard administrators, went about our business for a full week—this included informal socialization with all of the students—not least with members of the Third World Collective.

One week later we were re-called for a second plenary session.

The fellow who had announced the takeover rose. "The Third World Collective met and decided that you and Ed may resume your roles as leaders of the Goddard Graduate Program in communication with—and respect for—all of the students— particularly members of the Black and Hispanic Collective. How does that suit you?"

"Suits us," I said. "Delighted with your support. Now let's get to work."

An adventure in theater, perhaps. But one of a culturally serious sort in keeping with the revolutionary times.

Thus began the program. Conflict remained high on the activities agenda throughout, sometimes with students but more often with the Goddard College Administration.

And we hired at least a half dozen more faculty over the years—strong, interesting people who did well with our students.

The Ex-Con Contingent

The bulk of our students were much the same as adult students anywhere. They were attracted to Goddard because they appreciated the flexibility of independent study.

We, the faculty members, however, were always looking to increase the range of student needs, background and motivation.

I was approached by a fellow who had just been released from the Concord, Mass. State Prison. He had heard of our program through Jonathan Clark who had worked with me at Playroom 81. He now assisted the notorious Timothy Leary in running an intense and deeply appreciated substance-assisted weekly group for incarcerated volunteers.

The prisoners learned of our graduate program through Jonathan.

There is the story of a fellow who was about to be released after twenty-five years in prison. "What should I do when I get out?" he asked a recently released friend who was now a student in our program.

"First: Get fucked," the friend advised. "Second: Enroll in the Goddard Graduate Program."

From the point of view of the credibility of our Program, however, there was a problem: How might we justify admission for people who had no previous undergraduate experience? After some thought and discussion we concluded that a significant number of years in a maxim security prison such as Concord when combined with the intensive processing that occurred in Leary's group meetings arguably matches the learning that occurs in conventional university bachelor degree programs.

We soon had about a half dozen ex-cons enrolled. They all did good, serious work, most of it in having to do with helping other people—social and recreational involvements. One fellow embarked on a career teaching mentally retarded children. Another became a progressive political advocate. I have heard from two or three of them over the years. Sadly, I do not have records to refer to and cannot give a complete report. My recollection, however, is that there was little if any recidivism and little if any continued substance abuse.

We also had writers and artists come out of our graduate program as well as businesspeople, composers, executives, teachers, entertainers, political leaders, and adventurers.

This was a significant period in my professional life.

A happy interlude. Interesting, too.

But I was restless. Administrative work, creative or otherwise, was not really my thing. I wanted to get back to kids.

Counseling Camps

Impressed by the changes observed in children, even difficult ones, over a single summer's experience in one more reasonably good camp, I had for some years entertained the notion of developing my own therapeutic camp, partly for the good of the child but partly as a training ground for mental health workers.

One summer, I developed a personal and institutional relationship with The Morgan Memorial—Salvation Army—Fresh Air Camp in Western Massachusetts. I lived there with my family. My job was to supervise student volunteers in their work with campers who were for the most part poor kids from Boston. The students would receive course credit from their college plus a basic stipend.

About a half dozen undergraduate students signed up. The program seemed to work well with few if any hitches.

The task was not to do "therapy" with campers but rather to engage with an entire group—a cabin, a team, a gaggle of friends—and to participate naturally while being alert to precisely what was going on. We then had sessions in our student group to consider what was seen and sensed.

Mary, Alice and Michael lived at the camp, too. Our kids participated fully as campers.

The Morgan Memorial experience was for me a most attractive professional training/service model. And it was a motivating factor in accepting the job at Goddard College in rural Vermont.

Soon thereafter, I landed a lovely job at Goddard College while the Morgan Memorial experience was quite fresh in mind.

A Work in Progress

July 14, 2019: Happy Jour de la Bastille, Jules, *Mon Vieux!*

Thank you for your thoughtful critique of my beginning draft-memoir. I very much appreciate your kind words and intelligent perspective.

I see you as a fellow admirer of humanity in the context of the social, political and ethical turmoil in which we all are drowning.

Having read a number of your own thought-pieces, I see you as a fellow seeker of a warehouse, a trunk— at least an overnight bag —in which to deposit the accumulated wisdom of a long life so that it may serve to edify our progeny; hopefully for them to be instructed by us, to admire us, perhaps even to respect and emulate us, all improbable and creepy eventualities.

My writing is intended to examine the limits of my profession—insanity abatement— using stories from explorations in many contexts: summer camps, urban communities, Universities, Goddard, The Clearing and, on retirement, Russia and, finally, Haiti.

It all comes across, hopefully, as a celebration of convivial human community as context, even cure; supplementing, even supplanting, the studied techniques of interpersonal influence.

I am indebted to you for having read so many of my words and for having shared your own thoughts and suggestions.

Bob

The Clearing

It was somewhere with me for years, maybe always, certainly when Mary and I first began discussing the possibility of moving to Vermont.

But it had haunted me well before that when I worked with kids in Boston neighborhoods. And, yes, even much earlier while still at educationally sophisticated camps like Woodland and especially at Marcella, the New Jersey Camp for Blind Children.

The fantasy was to remove the child for a retreat from all that is familiar—relationships, houses, schools, streets, food, smells, relatives, friends, expectations and duties.

And to immerse him or her in a beautiful, remote, undeveloped but convivial hideaway from the world; and to remain there just long enough to re-imagine one's self into a new but familiar version of him or her own self, and with that self strengthening to accommodate the success of the accommodation, to return, stronger, to the original, familiar but hitherto problematic scene.

The idea was then to retreat periodically in order to to pull it all together, to gain strength, then to return home better for the experience.

Crazy?

While building the Goddard Graduate Program, I found time to scout the neighboring Vermont area to find attractive land for my camp project. I soon found a beautiful and affordable tract in a forest, close to a large lake and not far from the College.

David Sellers, a terrific young architect, was on the Goddard faculty at that time. I discussed my emerging plans with him. I said that we needed a structure for housing staff and kids, for feeding them, sleeping and having lots of space left for art, music, dance and discussions.

David's students designed just such a building, tall, modern but rustic. Immersed in the forest. A clearing. Two story wood house. A veranda. Two work rooms. Wood heat. An outhouse. Water to be brought up from the lake in buckets. A mile from the road. And a five minute bushwhack to the large lake.... standing tall among the trees of the forest.

Staff, one or two at a time, were primarily Goddard students plus an occasional student from Concordia University in Montreal where I taught for a while on a part time basis.

Kids appeared through local schools, Vermont social services, attorneys, parents or ... God knows how .... Many found their own way to us. We began with four or five regulars— which meant that they came on their own or we drove them to us every week or so.

Sessions varied from a few hours to one or two overnights.

There were periodic conflicts with social services. But we usually arrived at a modus vivendi.

To be a client of The Clearing was for some an honor, an achievement.

A friend created a t-shirt complete with a colorful "The Clearing" logo. A boy—long since deceased— was hauled into court for some delinquent act. I came with him.

"What is the significance of that logo on your t-shirt?" The judge asked.

"That," said the boy with evident pride, "is my club!" And so it was.

But the original house burned down a few years later in a terrible fire—stupidly accidental. No one was injured but it almost killed us all. We rebuilt thanks to insurance. Then fifteen years later a second fire consumed the second house. No one was there. So... once again we were able to build with insurance a third house, this one perhaps more beautiful but certainly more conventional than the earlier ones.

We had originally used oil lamps at night and hauled our water from the lake in buckets. Eventually, we installed solar electricity and dug a well on a hill with a pipe going to our kitchen and, one day, to an indoor bathroom as well.

I quit Goddard after eight years in favor of throwing myself into this experiment in therapeutic camping and the concomitant training of mental health students and young professionals—an ambitious but doable scheme.

Throughout, most of our campers were poor Vermont kids who found their way to us through public schools, social service agencies, and word of mouth. We also entertained occasional special groups from out of state.

Angela Searcy whom I had known as a child, daughter of Barbara Searcy, founder of Playroom 81, now a social work administrator, brought Boston kids to The Clearing for special sessions. We had a similar relationship with an agency in New York City.

And we had occasional prep school clients as well, kids as well as their affluent parents. Sometime these were combined with our regular clientele in a single session. Sometimes not.

From time to time, we also scheduled weekend visitation sessions with a kid and his or her non-custodial father.

All sorts of combinations and permutations. Constant experimentation... usually these were more or less successful judging from kid, parent, social worker or teacher comments.

I remember when a half-dozen black teen age girls from New York joined an outdoor square dance party in honky-white St. Johnsbury, Vermont. The high-spirited, rhythmic and arhythmic styles fused into a meld of two normally disparate cultures much to the hilarity and delight of all present.

Oh, and the animals! We kept two charming, eminently civilized donkeys at The Clearing both as pets and pack animals. They never bit or kicked and were great with children.

And we always had a child-oriented dog or two hanging around.

At first and occasionally for years to come, runaway children and teenagers showed up unannounced to establish or reestablish connection.

One cold winter day I hiked through the woods to check on something. I noticed a snowsuit hanging from the upstairs railing. The door was locked but a window had been left open. I entered—through the door—and noted that everything was in order. When I took a closer look at the snowsuit, I knew the owner at once, a little girl about ten years old who lived in public housing in nearby Barre.

Furious, I drove to see her.

"You broke into The Clearing!" I accused.

She looked surprised and broke into tears. "But you told us that it is our place," she cried. "So I did the dishes, swept the floors and put everything away."

She and her sister had bicycled twenty-two miles round trip to get there in addition to a two mile hike through the woods.

One might wonder how I made a living at this thing. The answers: "Not quite" and "In various ways." Prep school kids had parents. That helped. Out of state kids were occasionally at least somewhat sponsored by schools or agencies. Local self-referred kids often carried insurance, Medicaid ... or nothing at all. Non-custodial fathers kicked in out of pocket. One mother baked us a loaf of bread. It all worked out but I wouldn't say that we had a great business model.

And what exactly was I charging for? A kid might spend, say, six hours at The Clearing of which five were devoted to canoeing, swimming and hacking around. Maybe the remaining hour could be considered time spent my talking with him or her about personal or family problems. In that case, I would charge Medicaid for one hour professional time. Eighteen dollars. Fair enough.

Then one day, I received a letter from Vermont's Medicaid office. It stated that I was under investigation for Medicaid Fraud. Probable fine: $2,000.

Panicked, I hired the smartest, meanest attorney I knew, a guy who had once destroyed me on the stand when I was a witness for the opponent to his client.

Medicaid interviewed me and took a good look at my shame-fully chaotic records.

Months went by.

Then I received a second letter from Medicaid. This time it was clearly stated in lawyerly language that after a careful review it was concluded that they owed me one-thousand ($1,000.00) dollars!

Imagine that?

Part II

The Last Time I Saw Haiti

Gody in Action

September 30, 2010 Thursday

Entry #1 ... Why?

Though historically more isolated from the world than most, Haiti serves as an iconic case study of the relations between the Great Powers and the world's poor; easily exploitable people. In Haiti's case, this meant former slaves now merely poor folk, those in possession of things the Big Guys must have, including free labor, sugar, strategic location, and more recently, bauxite from which aluminum is produced.

Next item of importance: I broke my upper left canine tooth in Vermont the other day. Consultation with both a general dentist and a periodontist suggested that it will be a big deal to repair— including yanking, root canal, bone grafting and an implant. The cost will be in the neighborhood five thousand dollars of which as much as half might be covered by insurance.

I decided to get a second opinion from our former periodontist in Burlington but, since I am going to Haiti in less than a week, none of this can take place until I return. The local dentist stabilized the wiggling tooth with cement. But that was two days ago and it is coming loose again.

Can I possibly go to Haiti in such a condition? Wouldn't I be advised to remain home and suffer my tooth?

I try not to think of Haitians who survive in fragile tents blown away by autumn storms while suffering wounds, fractures, hunger, exposure to the elements, arbitrary death of friends and relations as well as untold psychic trauma.

And surely an occasional bad tooth.

The dentist handed me a prescription for antibiotics in case of trouble.

Entry #2—October 4, 2010

The Amtrak engine bumps and rattles to New York City from Washington, DC where Mary and I had attended a memorial to a friend. Then on to Haiti ... a world away ... although tomorrow at this time I will be preparing for landing at the Mais Gate Airport. What a spooky name, Mais Gate! It means "Rotten Corn." How is that for a prophesy?

It is raining heavily as the lumbering iron reptile traces the Northeast Corridor. Shall I say that this reflects sadness? For the friend we came to mourn in Washington? For the countless Haitians who lost their loved ones and homes in the recent catastrophe? Or is it of no significance at all, God having more than enough to do monitoring fallen sparrows ...?

Richard, my Haitian friend, long time smart guy, born in Haiti, spent his youth on the streets of New York and his grown years in Port-au-Prince; quick, knowledgeable, able to find what you want, speaks Creole like a Haitian and English like a New Yorker, one of the best of the Haitian Virgils, a guide to the many domains of Haiti's hell; heaven, too.

It is Richard who offered to bring together several ("Richard," I said, "no more than FOUR") people-of-the- streets-and-parks for me to interview. About what, he asked? I do not know, I replied, probably their lives.

The plan is to collect tales to tell back home in the benighted states. The most useful role that occurred to me is story-teller. Photographer, too. Perhaps I can bring about a glimmer of visibility to the unseen and unseeable.

I will meet the people, mostly teenagers, at the Cafe La Terrace, a homey establishment way up the hill in relatively middle class Petionville owned and operated by a US husband and wife team who have lived in Haiti for many years. Along the way they have quietly offered a meal to countless Haitians of the streets including the gritty, witty and obscene Holner La Tendresse, the recently deceased Grand Dame of the Sans Manmans ("without mothers," i.e. vagabonds) who enjoyed the company almost as much as the servings.

People will come, Richard warned me, for the food. I don't mind, I said, as long as they consent to honest interviews. But, thought I, journalists worth their salt never pay for interviews, do they? Will my free meals compromise what is said?

Who cares, I reply as long as the tales wag well.

Entry #3 October 6, 2010

The plane eases downward. I note the greenery adjacent to the runway and the tiny houses beyond which from a distance appear to be whitewashed and pretty. I can see the blue and white plastic of the tents that provides temporary housing for the displaced. The airport buildings seem unharmed. In fact, a major expansion of the airport appears to be in progress. But I am agitated in anticipation of what lies ahead.

We disembark along one of those long, portable, enclosed corridors common throughout the world in major airports. Retrieving baggage is a frustrating hassle here but scarcely more so than at JFK, Logan, LA, or anywhere.

Carla met me in a four-wheel-drive car along with three other passengers, all Haitians. Carla and her husband, Ron, are white Americans. They have lived in Haiti for over thirty years.

They and their close Haitian friends formed an educational organization, "N a Sonje," We Will Remember. It presents Haitian history in song and theater to journalists and diplomats; tourists, too.

We drove to their home compound high in the mountains beyond Petionville in the scraggly town of Gwo Jan, "Fat John." The destruction caused by the earthquake was only rarely seen here.

Haiti itself generally seemed to be much as I had known it for lo! these many years. About thirty. Remarkable... but, as I soon was to learn, untrue. Haiti is always changing, sometimes for the better; often for the worse.

I was exhausted, not having slept much the night before. I had needed to catch the Super Shuttle from Vermont to JFK at four-thirty A.M. Yet when we got to her home, Carla and I talked and talked on into what seemed the dawn but was actually only seven-thirty pm. Then I collapsed into bed and did not stir until six-thirty am whereupon we yammered some more and yet more. The conversation was largely about Haitian culture and history as reflected in the character of individuals as well as in the politics of society.

At midday Carla drives me to La Terrace Cafe in Petionville to meet my buddy, Richard, that smart New York Haitian man of many streets, insightful but neither blatantly dishonest nor actually a criminal sort.

I am convinced that Richard is a valuable asset for this very foreign country. He is a man of two cultures. Born in Haiti, then as a little kid he and his mom emigrated to the States. He grew up in New York.

Finally, as a young man devoid of citizenship, he was removed to Haiti where he found loneliness as well as occasional employment as guide and translator;

seldom lucrative work but sufficient to feed himself and always interesting.

A helpful fellow. One day I missed my flight back to the States. The next flight was sold out. Richard took me to the airline offices and quickly negotiated a fine seat for me ordinarily reserved for airline executives.

In any case, I invited Richard to be one of my best post-apocalypse Haitian Virgils.

****

Summary of today's main event: I spent an hour or two running many ideas by both Carla and Richard both of whom generally approved and provided me with helpful feedback.

Entry #4 Thursday, October 7, 2010. Gwo Jan/Big John

Six twenty-six in the morning. The sound of rushing water in the brook some few yards from the house. Everyone snores. I woke an hour ago. The dawn air is warm but not oppressively so. It rained last night as it has each night for many weeks, I am told. Rain is welcome in this scorched country.

Neither bugs, flies, nor mosquitoes announce themselves although there are no screens on the windows and doors. Strange. Is Haiti too poor to feed its insects?

We are in the mountains high over Port-au-Prince just beyond Petionville, an affluent suburb. Not far to the city. Gwo Jan, too, is something like a suburb. Yet it feels very remote. One must travel a long, scarcely maintained dirt road to get here. Carla explained that in a country where almost no one owns a vehicle, there is little motivation to keep a road in shape.

A cock crows. A dog barks. Otherwise, silence.

After lunch, Richard accompanied me on a sight-seeing venture around Petionville. We strolled through the large camp where hundreds of refugees from January's earthquake were squatting right by the city hall in the relatively elite town center. People squat there in extremely close proximity to each another.

Just opposite the city hall is a famous church; and across the street is the elegant Kinam Hotel, still standing and still host to visiting NGO officials, the international press, military brass, missionaries, hustlers and consultants.

There are no tourists in Haiti anymore.

Strangely, the post-disaster refugee scene is unremarkable. It has the feel of permanence about it. Children play, women hang out laundry on strings and lampposts, sidewalk vendors display their wares of fruits, vegetables, miscellaneous hardware and old clothes. A temporary bandstand was set up in the center of the camp. Music groups perform. Except for one guy who aggressively demanded ten dollars—American— from me, no beggars approached us nor did we seem the objects of curiosity. There were no police in evidence although we did note a temporary, wooden structure with a sign on it indicating that it housed the "Ministry for the Protection of Haitian Women."

This is an instant Haitian village, one of many, perhaps more crowded than most but indistinguishable from the others. Except for the fact that people live in tents rather than houses and that many of these are frayed or torn and that they are set on ground that turns to mud in the rain arriving every evening, it is a very ordinary place, no longer elite; familiar and likely to remain so for god knows how long.

Richard was amazed, he said, that the camp had not yet been devastated by disease.

Unfortunately, Richard never did find anybody for me to interview. Partly my fault. We were chatting and he forgot. So did I.

Carla and I spoke this morning and yesterday as well about what she calls the "crabs in a barrel" phenomenon. It is said that if you put a bunch of crabs in a barrel and one of them tries to escape by climbing up the inside, the others will pull it back down. That, Carla said, is the model of what happens when an individual Haitian attempts to pull him or herself away from the community toward individual advancement. The community will yank him right down again.

At the same time, I should think, this would make the role of the community leader, the big guy, the Gwo Neg, that much more attractive, conferring on such a person considerable prestige along with power over others. It might also represent the roots of reputed Haitian inertia on the one hand and rampant corruption on the other. If there is no power to adjudicate intra-community conflicts, those who nonetheless rise tend to do so through the very embodiment of self-serving chicanery.

Much that we see in the Haitian character may be traced to the history of slavery and subsequent exploitation. One may note placidity on the one hand overlaying a strong communitarian ethos and a substrate under both of jealousy and an obsessive scratching for position and personal survival. Yet Haiti is also a country of saints, remarkable people who sacrifice their health, comfort and gain for the benefit of others.

Amateur social science perhaps, yet with a muffled ring of truth.

It is the saints who attract and baffle me. Although fury and cruelty are often manifest, is the fundamental decency, generosity, selflessness and kindness that is evident in the Haitian character that simply blows me away.

What could possibly account for that?

Entry #5 October 7, 2010

I am now in a guest house in the Delmas neighborhood of downtown Port-au-Prince. I signed out of N a Sonje earlier today in favor of being closer to the one orphanage with which I am still involved, "Le Foyer des Filles de Dieu," a humane, responsible yet traditional place ("silence when eating!") run by the indomitable Mme Paula Thybulle, who is Haitian "Mulatto"— a word that seems to connote "upper class and disinterested" within the great sea of poor people in which everyone here is immersed. But Mme Paula, despite her position and politics, does not fit the stereotype. She has devoted her life to the children under her care and, although stern when she needs to be, she has a famous heart of gold. The girls call her "Manman Paula."

Mme Paula is a naturalized US citizen and has lived for some twenty-five years in the New York area. She was trained in the States as a social worker. She eventually returned to Haiti to serve abandoned and abused children. She has devoted her life to them. Mme Paula is a saint in the eyes of many, foremost among them the girls in her care.

The pensionne where I now reside is only a few blocks from Mme Paula's Le Foyer. My thought was to visit tomorrow. But just a few minutes ago I phoned to let her know my plans. She answered in a weak voice and informed me that she is in the hospital, brought there today. For what was unclear.

I then spoke with Paula's friend, the Paris-trained physician, Dr. La Planche, who is director of a community health clinic affiliated with the orphanage. Dr. La Planche said that Paula is probably suffering from pneumonia.

I am very concerned, concerned for Paula but even more so for her girls. I cannot imagine what will happen to them if Paula should find herself unable to function.

I will visit the orphanage tomorrow morning to see how the girls are doing. Their residence has been destroyed by the earthquake, Dr. La Planche said. But almost everyone was in the yard by the gate at the time. Therefore, no one was in the building when it collapsed. Three girls, however, were off visiting the orphanage cook at her home which also collapsed. All three—plus the cook and her family—were killed.

I will talk again with Dr. LaPlanche tomorrow and somehow get to the hospital to see Paula. It will be a long day. Then my plan after the orphanage is to visit programs in the city of Leogane, an ancient, relatively small but busy metropolis that was the epicenter of the earthquake. I anticipate horror. Leogane is reputed to be where the Voudon religion began.

En route to the guest house, Carla drove me to the offices of Fonkoze, a major US-Haiti NGO. I conferred there with Ann

Hastings, the local—white American—head of that organization. I wanted to see if it might be possible in the future for Fonkoze to become fiscal agent for the various groups with which I am acquainted. I left Ann's office convinced that it not only would be possible but would in fact be a very good thing to do. From Northern New England I simply cannot perform the fiscal or programmatic "due diligence" that is required after making a donation.

To be of use, I need to know which organizations it is best to support and in return require a report from them at the end of the year indicating just how the money was spent. We also need a programmatic evaluation to provide some sense of the effectiveness of the program, gift or intervention.

Since the end of the Aristide regime there has been no government worth talking about in Haiti. We are thus reduced to working through the best Non-Governmental Organization we can find. One that has its nose to the ground.

Carla then drove me through the great tangle of traffic in downtown Port-au-Prince. We did not happen to pass the government and financial center that has reportedly been entirely destroyed, "a message from God," as they say here. But we did go down Avenue Grand Delmas and through side streets many of which were familiar to me for years. We also visited two of Carla's Haitian friends who live as organizers in a tent encampment.

Destruction was everywhere, some dramatic as in the utter elimination of The Caribbean Market, an American style supermarket, killing many shoppers and clerks.

Some buildings were untouched. But what stood out for me was the steady drumbeat of collapsed house here and another there, rocks, chips of cement and trash uncollected, probable buried bodies left as they fell, ignored.

Thousands of people perished. No one can say how many.

Yet throngs of people continue about their daily business, chatting, walking, carrying loads in their hands or on their heads. Once again, I felt the incongruous presence of the workaday world.

Carla and I bade each other farewell. She is a fine hostess. She and Ron, her husband, have done singular intercultural work for many years in this country, They are white, expatriot Americans with no plans for returning to the States. Despite everything, they believe that Haiti is culturally a healthier place in which to live than is the US.

Ann Hastings, the key figure in Fonkoze, is also a white American who has lived here for a long time. She and Carla have similar feelings. Her work brings her to the States often. But once having completed her tasks and visiting her grandchildren, she hurries back to Haiti.

Haiti is a wonderful and a terrible country. It is currently experiencing one of the most corrupt political periods in its ghastly history and yet ... and yet ... and yet there remains something enormously attractive about the place. It casts a Voudon spell,

I have just signed into Walls' Guest House which is overflowing with missionaries. I have no idea how many; certainly well over a dozen. They don't seem annoying in the sense of pushing their particular god, an enterprise that does not prove difficult in a country with so many gods—another one or two surely does no harm. But these particular Americans are just so ... how can I put it? ... so classically American: Overweight, wearing shorts and sports shirts, they guzzle beer and yammer and guffaw and carry themselves with well advertised authority. Their purpose, one of them told me, is to build houses for the homeless, a great idea on the face of it.

But first, who told them that Haitians require American-sponsored labor? Haitians tend to be sufficiently competent and hardworking though chronically unemployed.

In the second place, how do these folks presume that the design of their contributions will meet Haitian needs? I mean, how well do they know local conditions? About as well, I suspect as we know the needs and conditions of Afghanis, Iranians, Iraqis and Africans.

Around the next table from me four blans[6] are discussing how they plan to conduct the construction project. The fellow who seems technically the best informed is holding forth.

What he is proposing is a house with a tin roof. I had earlier asked him if a tin roof would not transmit heat to the people under it. Might not insulation of some sort help, I wondered? He explained that the tin reflects the sun's heat and that the roof would be so constructed as to leave a gap between the two halves. Heat would flow right out. "It is easily ten degrees cooler on the inside under these conditions than on the outside," he said. The intention is to instruct Haitians on his design. He also claimed that his houses will be earthquake and hurricane resistant.

---

[6]whites

But what I did not ask him—being ready for a nap—is why not check this out with an occasional Haitian? Although in Port-au-Prince and other cities, people have been building concrete houses with cement roofs advertising wealth, solidity and permanence, one finds that in the hustings, thatched roof, pole-frame buildings have been in fashion for centuries, millennia if you include Africa. Such structures are remarkable in that they remain cool inside, can be constructed with local materials and by local labor. Plus they are flexible whether in the face of a hurricane or a massive earthquake.

The key advantage in my view is that such buildings are made entirely through the efforts of the local community thus strengthening interpersonal bonds.

Americans famously have a tendency to march right in with a take-charge attitude. The result is often a high tech solution well beyond the means of ordinary people and one that requires plenty of cash for parts and products manufactured in the United States.

Shameful, I say. Shameful.

The Russian word, "samadour," is applicable. It refers to someone with a take-charge attitude who doesn't have a clue as to what he (or she) is talking about.

Along with missionary Americans perhaps a dozen Haitians live in this guest house, some as transients. I suspect that most are employed as cooks, guards and cleaning women. My room is close to their living section which contains several memorable scenes. One family has two little kids, girls, one around three and the other perhaps one. Cute, cheerful children and very well behaved.

It is refreshing to live among aliens.

Entry #6 October 8, 2010

I am in Leogane. It is the founding center of the Voudon religion. The recent earthquake rendered this city utterly devastated. Leogane was the epicenter. The Haitian guys who drove me here were astounded by the destruction ... and they live in Port au Prince which was hardly spared.

But Leogane is worse off on many levels. Rue La Croix— where the Gateau Guest House once stood and where its empty shell still may be seen—is flattened. Every house is gone, completely gone. Rubble. A pile of broken cement walls, pebbles and sand. I once knew the street but now could not decide exactly where it had been. A nightmare.

Yet where I am now sitting it is otherwise. Tranquil... even though tents for displaced families surround us.

Yoleine Gateau-Esposito is co-director and co-founder along with James Philemy of "the NEGES Foundation," a local NGO. Both are Haitian-Americans who live in Brooklyn and work for the New York City Board of Education yet manage to be in Leogane as often as once a month.

Thanks to the flattening of their entire operation in the town's center, they are in the process of moving everything a mile or so into the country to "Mon Petit Village." That is where I sit at the moment.

It is where we held an American volunteer work camp five years ago the purpose of which was to transform old automobile tires into planters for trees and bushes.

Now it is full of people, tents and laundry drying in the sun.

In the sheltered "kiosk," where we had once gathered for celebrations and meetings, teenagers—most of them boys; one, a girl—are practicing karate moves while dressed in white uniforms. They run, jump, kick and punch. The performance— much like a classic dance routine—is highly disciplined. We sit on the porch of the main house watching as we discuss the miracle of the new iPod Touch especially if used with a cool Bluetooth keyboard like the one I am now using.

Several of the young men here, especially a certain "John"— probably "Jean"—and another guy whose name I didn't catch, are very well informed technologically. It is remarkable that in a low-tech country like Haiti—especially in a remote area such as this—we find cyberwise young people who are conversant in all sorts of high-tech matters.

So there we were discussing iPods and wireless internet connections and Bluetooth keyboards. One of the guys, Edy, even has an iPhone of his own, albeit a damaged one that doesn't quite work. It was given to him by a friend. We discussed the advantages and disadvantages of network-based telephone systems such as Skype versus those with cell phone company contracts.

* * *

I had spoken with Mme Paula Thybulle on the phone this morning and with her friend and physician, Dr. LaPlanche, in person before I left for Leogane. Paula is feeling better now and should be okay soon.

Unfortunately, I had not managed to visit Paula. What with the traffic and the rubble ahead, it would have taken the whole day. Instead I had dropped in on the orphanage, Le Foyer des Filles de Dieu, to say "goodbye." The girls were happy to see me: they wanted to know if I had come to take them to the beach. I told them that it depended on Mme Paula and the needs of the orphanage.

I waited around for Dr. LaPlanche. She is co-director of Le Foyer with Mme Paula. She has particular responsibility for the affiliated community health clinic. But she also takes an interest in the functioning of the entire operation. Dr. LaPlanche is an attractive, stylishly dressed, middle aged woman. She is light-skinned, educated in France and has more the manner of an elite European than a Haitian. She is gracious and professional rather than overtly warm.

While hanging out, I spent my time lounging in the courtyard with children all around me, touching my skin admiringly, sitting on my lap, poking me, asking questions, looking at pictures on my iPod, taking a few more with my camera, but most of all just sitting very close both to me as well as to one another.

A girl introduced her sisters, one ten and the other, seven.

She herself is eleven.

"How long have you kids been here?" I asked.

"Two years," she said.

"And why did you come?"

"Our mother died of fever. And our father had no work. He could not take care of us."

"It is sad to lose a mother," I ventured. "You must miss her."

"We do."

"Do you take care of each other."

"We do."

"Do you like it here?"

"We do."

I finally met with Dr. LaPlanche who was worried about the fiscal state of the orphanage. Paula is responsible for seventy-two children but has barely enough money to feed them. She was not able to send them to school this week for lack of funds and is concerned about next week when again the prospect of getting them to school seems remote.

Dr. LaPlanche believes that Mme Paula's illness was precipitated by the extreme financial stress that she has been under.

I explained that when I take the children to the beach it costs me about three hundred dollars. I have about five hundred dollars with me for this part of my trip. Perhaps, I suggested, it would be more helpful if I were simply to hand it to the orphanage so that the children can attend school next week. Dr. LaPlanche agreed—of course. She assigned a young man, a staff member, to accompany me to the hotel where I wrote out a check for five hundred dollars which he then brought to Dr. LaPlanche.

Just prior to leaving, I said to a group of girls, "Sadly, the orphanage needs money so that you can go to school next week. I think it is more important that you go to school than that you go to the beach. Don't you?"

They stared at me silently. A few nodded their heads. They were not convinced. Dr. LaPlanche promised to discuss the matter with them later.

Leogane—continued: Someone at the guest house in Port au Prince had found a guy who was willing to transport me to Leogane at a fair price—$100 US. The driver, Bruce, brought his friend, John, along with him. Both are friendly fellows. John speaks some English and so-so French which, he said, he learned on his own. Bruce speaks only Creole.

It took several hours to navigate the thirty or so miles from Port-au-Prince to Leogane. The roads were replete with pot holes and crevices. For much of the trip, a fog of dust and sand particles hung over everything. Traffic jams were continual. Neighborhoods I had known—Bizoton, Carrefour, Mariani, Belleville—were reduced to rubble and dust.

The two driver guys asked me for the address of the guest house. "62, rue La Croix," I said.

We tried to find it. But the street itself no longer existed. Dust and rubble was all that remained. It was then that I fully understood the astounding destruction to the City of Leogane.

I shall return tomorrow to photograph the scene and to interview anyone I meet.

Destroyed by the earthquake, the guest house had moved to the countryside. It was now reestablished in "Mon Petit Village," a mile or so from Leogane. Mon Petit Village is an incipient, fully Haitian, utopian community.

Entry #7: The next day. 8:28 AM

I am ensconced in Mon Petit Village. It is morning. I slept well. The shower was excellent although it offered only cold water. But in tropical climes, cold water is actually sort of warm by subjective standards.

Last night, I met Molly, my fellow guest, a teenage adventurer from the US; a friend of my grandson's once girlfriend.

Molly and I chatted with Jocelyn who in turn is the best friend —"we are like sisters"—of Yoleine, the director of the NEGES Foundation, a US non-governmental organization that runs Mon Petit Village. Jocelyn was standing in for Yoleine who is currently in Brooklyn doing her job as Director of Guidance. She returns to Haiti often.

Jocelyn had lived in the US for many years but has always longed to return to Haiti. "I love it here," she said. "I am simply not into the American Dream."

Jocelyn is a "Mambo," a Voudon priestess, the title suggesting that she is a very powerful woman who has received a call from the spirits.

We covered topics of these sorts on into the night—actually it was only about eight-thirty when I hit the sack—but it felt much, much later.

Morning

Everything is delightful and nicely functioning in Mon Petit Village. Morning. Roosters crow and dogs bark, my favorite concert pieces.

The boys are up early, in uniform and yet again busy practicing Karate. They are quick and fierce and accompany each move with impressive grunts and shouts. The women have prepared a simple breakfast for us and are sweeping the yard.

One old woman is, unasked, doing my laundry—which I could (of course) do myself. There is even a washing machine in the house. She is working gratis, she said, but I figured it better to pay her. Cheaper all around, and good for her—and the environment. The gasoline required to power the generator that works the washing machine might well cost about the same as the ten dollars I will pay her.

I am off to my photographic assignment

Entry #8 October 9, 2010

"The Photographic Assignment" turned out to be rather different than I had anticipated. Ricardo, one of the guys who hang around here, an earnest, pleasant fellow, asked Molly and me if we would like to visit an orphanage down the road. He used to work there, he explained, and added something to the effect that he himself had been raised in an orphanage although not that particular one. We were curious and so agreed but I added a caveat that I was not about to hand out money nor was I in a position to adopt anybody.

Ricardo hailed two motorcycle taxis. He and Molly hopped on one and I mounted the other. Off we went five or so miles down the road to the "Lamb Missionary Orphanage" where we spent the better part of the morning.

Like most orphanages in Haiti, it is run by some Protestant church. But this one is Haitian—not American—sponsored. The Pastor introduced himself but his name didn't stick in my mind; unfortunately I neglected to jot it down.

I tend to be allergic to pastors but this one didn't seem so bad. There was something reasonable about the guy. He did not attempt to press his religion on me and was convincingly concerned with the welfare of the children. But who can say?

Orphanages are big business in Haiti as they are in much of the world. And abuse is often rife.

The children stood staring at us with sad eyes and endearing faces. There are thirty-six kids in the Pastor's care between the ages of, I judge, three and fourteen. There is a staff of nineteen, and no permanent building. Everyone lives in tents donated by UNICEF and USAID. The Pastor, cleanly dressed, competent in manner, explained that they do not have enough money to run the place properly. He showed me where the pump house had been until utterly destroyed by the earthquake .

"We need to send the children on a hike down the road to UNICEF with plastic milk jugs for water," he said. "Otherwise, is impossible for them to take proper baths or wash clothes and they barely have enough left to drink. We don't have sufficient funds to feed them well or to pay our staff adequate salaries. Sadly, we are not affiliated with a partner church in the United States.

We get a little help from UNICEF but it is not enough." I was surprised that he never asked me for money.

We played with the children. I took many pictures—some quite moving—then the staff gathered everyone in the yard and had us all sing songs together and play party games.

It was painful to leave them. Molly said that she would volunteer to work here one or two days a week.

After a couple of hours, we left to see Lorene's baby. They live not far from the orphanage in a one room perch that she rented from a sympathetic family.

Lorene is a young woman who was raised in another local orphanage, a cold, dreary place that I visited several years ago. When she reached age eighteen she was unceremoniously tossed out because they needed her bed. Yoleine, a tough woman with a famously soft heart, took her in temporarily. But now she is on her own.

Lorene has no skills, not even those of the most basic sort. She is emotionally needy and extremely vulnerable having had no experience in the world beyond the walls of an institution. She soon became pregnant by a guy she hardly knew.

A Vermonter friend of mine, "Andrea," took pity on Lorene during a visit. Andrea has sent her presents, funded her through a complicated pregnancy and now pays the rent for the room where she and her baby, a healthy seven month-old and healthy, now live.

Lorene named the baby "Andre" in honor of Andrea. Andrea refers to Lorene as "my daughter."

We returned to "Mon Petit Village" by Tap-Tap—

Haitian bus— followed by a short motorcycle ride. I spent the afternoon hiking to town and back— three or four mile—to photograph the destruction ... dramatic, extensive and infinitely sad.

I had brief encounters with many people along the way—children mostly—who wanted to know who I was and why I was there. I purchased a fine straw hat, essential in a country where the sun seems to blaze inches above one's head. The hat merchant woman asked who I was visiting.

On returning to Mon Petit Village, I was told that Molly had taken off down the busy highway on a bicycle that some of the local young guys had put together for her. That was several hours ago. Interesting news but hardly worrisome. It was only about four in the afternoon.

But by six Molly had still not returned and it was getting dark. Jocelyn, in charge here in Yoleine's absence, dispatched Markendy, a brilliant but marginally educated young man, to go to town on his motorcycle to find her. He returned an hour later to report that he was unsuccessful.

It is morning now. Molly returned sometime after I fell asleep.

We Americans are an odd lot, although obsessed with security to the extent that we kill for it, we nonetheless go through life oblivious to real danger, convinced in our soul that we are immortal.

Haitians by contrast live with the immediacy of death, respect its inevitability and develop skills to handle daily contingencies. They engage in a respectful dialogue with death's eternal, dreadful presence.

Entry #9 October 10, 2010

Molly woke up early, hopped on her bike and headed off. But this time she told Jocelyn approximately where she was going and when she would return.

I walked to Leogane somewhat later to change money. Even though it is Sunday, Pharmacie St. Michel is open and, according to Jocelyn, offers the best rate.

On the way I ambled about taking more pictures. When people asked who I was, I told them that I am a journalist ... which is close to the truth.

As I started back to Le Petit Village, Molly rode up, bright and cheery. We had a cool fruit drink together at a stand that consisted of a single small, plastic cooler. Treat was on Molly.

She told me that she and Jocelyn discussed her behavior and that she now realizes that she was in error not to have told anybody when she intended to return.

I said that the concern we all felt was partially for her well being but it was also organizational. If there are accidents or problems with people who volunteer with NEGES, its reputation becomes damaged both locally and internationally. A good reputation is critical for its existence.

Molly seems to have understood but she is a very independent sort who feels that she can handle anything. She will probably be okay in the long run ... but being responsible for her—which I am not— would likely be a full time occupation.

* * *

I am wandering the streets of Leogane once again, alone and feeling perfectly safe, taking pictures, engaging in brief inter-changes with an occasional passerby, simply sitting and observing the passing scene ... so many people living in tents, white tents, presumably to reflect the heat which is formidable in this area, far more so than in Petionville where I visited the other day or up in Lavale where I will be on Tuesday. Both have the advantages of high mountains. Leogane is at torrid sea level.

I find it hard to do much before I need to stop, drink water, take a nap and, if I am lucky, a shower as well. It is a slow, useless existence. Most Haitians seem to walk slowly here, often carrying things on their heads—the women especially. Both sexes work very hard.

I stood watching while a work crew formed a human chain to bring water up a long ladder to the roof of a building that was being reconstructed. The buckets were heavy but the men kept hauling them, rapidly, bucket after bucket, continuing for the longest time, sweat pouring from their naked backs, singing, shouting, in concert, perhaps even cheerfully but without rest; a team, an opera, a ballet.

People live in occasional undamaged houses but many more have settled into tents, some manufactured and contributed by such NGOs as UNICEF and USAID but many are slapped together ramshackle affairs.

The other day when I was without my camera I saw four people sitting under two upended mattresses that leaned upright against each other thus leaving a triangular space underneath as with cards. It was gone today when I returned to record it.

Some people have knocked pieces of scrap wood together to form a place to live; others have done a competent job of carpentry and have created a tiny but genuine house for themselves.

There are problems, however, one that was pointed out to me by the two guys who drove me here. It is this: Prior to the earthquake, most people had been paying rent for their living space. Living as they do now, hot, wet, minimal and uncomfortable though it may be, they pay nothing. Gratis. Furthermore, they are often given free electricity—or steal it—and are also recipients of food and supplies donated by international organizations and foreigners of good will.

Thus it is claimed, that many people do not actually wish to be rehabilitated. They prefer to stay right where they are.

And the government is so weak as to be virtually nonexistent. There is no one to persuade or require them to be or to live other than as they are now.

* * *

It is Sunday. Not much going on. This evening, though, there is to be a Voudon demonstration event. Jocelyn, among other things, is a Voudon priestess, a genuine "Mambo."

Should be interesting.

Entry #9: October 11, 2010

I have a few moments to relax so I shall record an especially fine episode.

But first: David.

Molly found this guy, David, a Canadian computer geek and amateur economist, an odd, goose-necked fellow who goes to places like Haiti on his own, NGO free, where he attempts to do good works. Molly finds him interesting. He is.

And he is smart. David is highly critical of the work that NGOs do and skeptical that they do anything much except raise money which then goes to purchase American-made products or serves to line the pockets of their administrators. His critique is similar to my own but he is better informed and way crankier.

Take the matter of the tents. People steal these, David explained, and sell them at odious prices to others even though they were obtained for nothing. Whatever is donated may become fuel for corruption. And the NGOs, with their heads in the clouds and noses farther still from the ground, have no idea what is actually going on and seem to care less thus opening the door to unbridled anarchy.

David's solution for post-catastrophe intervention whether in Haiti or elsewhere is simply to hand people hard cash to enable them to purchase whatever they wish. Period. Much more efficient than donating goods because transport would be rendered unnecessary as would armies of bureaucrats.

I found the idea attractive but am sure there must something wrong with it. Maybe it's that it smells of socialism and as such would never fly in the US. Or perhaps I don't trust people, any people, and suspect that they would use the money to purchase junk and starve happily.

Or, that with free money available, prices would rise accordingly and astronomically.

Now, the episode: After lunch and a nap, I strolled down a very basic dirt road for a hundred yards or so from where we are staying. Tethered cows munched contentedly in the fields, rice grew high, and grey-green mountains framed the horizon.

People greeted me as I ambled. "Hello. How are you, M'su? Good afternoon. Where are you from?" I got into several amiable conversations. A bit of begging was involved but it was light and good humored.

I took many pictures mostly of the scenery.

A young woman with a little girl at her side stopped me. "My house collapsed," she said. "Do you want to see how we must live?"

She led me behind a couple of tents, one white and the other blue. She pointed to the few rocks scattered on the ground.

"This is where my house was," she said as her little girl, Manushka, age five, clutched my leg and looked at me, grinning in the most endearing manner.

The mother, whose name was Miriam, continued. "I am twenty-four years old. I have another child, a son, who is ten. He and Manushka go to a Christian school. I must pay for that.

"Our tent"—she pointed to the white tent behind us—"is hot day and night. When it rains, the floor turns to mud. I barely have enough money to buy food."

I noted that Manushka had a protruding belly button, one of many signs of malnutrition.

Manushka was so cute—her smiles, her pigtails, her insistence on hugging my leg—that I found myself saying, "I have a little gift for you, Manushka. It is in my room at Mon Petit Village. You might like it. Wait right here and I will bring it to you in just a few minutes."

As soon as I said that I knew I had made a mistake. A harmless gift to someone in a poverty-stricken country can cause a riot. But, once having promised, I persevered. I returned to my room and retrieved two Zutanomade toy bunnies. The second was a spare in case another child were to show up. I brought them both to Manushka and gave one to her.

Sure enough, a three year old boy was visiting; a cousin, I recall.

"A girl rabbit for you, Manushka," I said. "And a boy rabbit for you," I told the little boy whose name did not remain in my head long enough to report. Both kids were delighted. Naturally

"Let's keep this a secret between us," I suggested. "These are all I have."

Manushka, dancing excitedly up and down, waved goodbye as I walked back down the road to Mon Petit Village.

Entry #10 October 11. Morning. 6:20AM

There was a Voudon show here last night. It was not an actual religious ceremony but rather an authentic show for foreigners, a first rate performance including music, dance and the drawing of a complex "veve"—sacred symbols drawn in corn meal on the ground.

A real Voudon seance would have been secret, not open to outsiders except under very special circumstances.

In this case, seven American women arrived in the afternoon. Most were students from Duke university. Five came as volunteers through some Christian organization determined to be useful in the area of maternal and child health. The two others were staff of both the university and the charity. The ceremony was in honor of the entire group.

The drumming, the singing and the dancing were at a very high level. There was little light, however, thus rendering photography difficult but I recorded the sounds on my iPod. I think one can experience a good sense of the event by listening to it.

The volunteers have been collecting stories from survivors of the earthquake. They are impressed with the resilience of the Haitian people. I am, too. One gets a clear sense of Haitian character strength by attending to folklore as we did last night.

The music and dance reflected an extraordinarily complex yet powerfully unified culture. Each voice can be heard, some occasionally rising above the rest, but the threads come together to create a single, multi-tonal fabric. It is the same with dance. Each person did his or her own step but the steps came together and interacted with one another to offer an occasionally ferocious, almost military unity constantly interspersed with witty variations. The shadows of jazz roots were obvious.

Haiti houses at once the most communal culture imaginable yet at the same time it seems utterly chaotic to the uninitiated. The two extremes exist in the same space and at the same time rendering Haiti impossible for the foreigner, me in this instance, to comprehend the entirety.

Sometimes I think that Haitians can't make full sense of it either.

In conversation with Jocelyn the other day she exclaimed that "this country needs a dictator." What a remarkable thing to say, I thought. And this from a most democratically inclined person! The remark was made in the context of a discussion about a British group that was here to organize the survivor camps.

"Why are foreigners needed to organize the camps?" I asked. "Surely, Haitians are capable of organizing themselves more effectively."

"Haitians are incapable of organizing themselves," Jocelyn said. "They are too competitive. Each person is out for himself."

Yet in another conversation, she is a person who proudly advertises the unity of the Haitian people.

This complexity may also be seen in the international volunteers.

There is a temptation to separate one's self from the NGOs— which are often faulted to be sure—and to go it on one's own, developing projects here and there and being useful where one can albeit in tiny venues.

I am like that or was. David, the fellow with whom we talked yesterday also seems to take that position. It has the advantage of keeping one's nose to the ground. But the downside is that it adds up to very little. No structures are left behind and the scale is so small as to make no real difference to the community—to say nothing of the country—as a whole.

Better, I think, to work with the best and largest organization one can and use ones training and insights to create something programmatic and effective on a grand scale, something that might relate to the communitarian side of Haitian culture but at the same time could satisfy the needs of the individual in a manner that would result in something beyond selfishness.

We withdraw to the micro level in our country. But in Haiti, a fragmented country, the tendency leads to even more feckless behavior. At times I think that Haiti is the crystal ball in which we see America's future. The only difference is that the US does not have an underlying agriculture-based, co-equal communitarian tradition.

Entry #12 October 11, 2010. Afternoon.

My life in Haiti is now routine. Each morning after breakfast I go off on an adventure, return for lunch and spend the afternoon, first with a nap and then a second shower of the day, insensitive of me perhaps given the uncertainty of the water supply here but I find it a necessary lapse. White skin privilege shall we call it?

Reason: I get extremely hot in this sea level Haitian city—as does everyone. So, I take a cold (coolish) shower on awaking each morning. No harm in that, I suppose, but I also permit myself the obscene luxury of a second rinse in mid afternoon.

Unfortunately, it is now almost two o'clock and our lunch has not yet been set out for us. Probably that is because the Duke University crew has gone and there is no food left in the house. Hunger, I suppose, gives me an unparalleled opportunity to express my solidarity with Haitians but I get no pleasure from it.

I hiked to town this morning yet again and spent some time observing in the reputedly enlightened NEGES elementary school that is currently housed in tents in the back yard of the blue building that was its pre-earthquake home. The experience fit seamlessly with last night's Voudon show and the subsequent discussions we had about "the Haitian character" and how to help Haiti get its act together.

167

Now it all makes sense.

The answer is clearly school. Schooling is responsible for the ills we find here in this hauntingly beautiful but traumatized country. No question about it. School is the culprit, perhaps more so than the earthquake.

I am not kidding.

Let me put it this way: This particular school is probably the best of what is offered the Haitian poor. It was founded by educators critical of the traditional system, people influenced by such as Maria Montessori and Howard Gardner. They wanted to establish something that would give the young generation the intellectual equipment to make a difference.

So we see children in these classrooms who, unlike those in traditional schools, work around tables and sit on chairs that are not fixed in place. Although they wear uniforms, there is a refreshing informality about the place—at least on the surface.

It is in the actual operation of the classroom that the problem becomes apparent. The pedagogy is not unlike those in the more typical schools, run in soporific style and painful to observe... even for sympathetic observers like myself and Molly who was with me for part of the time.

The children are passive recipients of pap and nonsense presented in a language that they don't understand. Their own language is Creole but the language of instruction is French.

In a classroom for very small children, two young teachers strolled from child to child repeating over and over and over again—in French: "How nice it is to be in school." They must have said it a thousand times. Young eyelids grew heavy, heads nodded, kids needed to be shaken awake.

They were taught no French songs, no French conversation, no French jokes. Nothing at all in Creole. Only that deadly foreign phrase.

In another classroom—one for older children—a textbook chapter covered the conquest of the Americas by the Europeans. What fine opportunity for a classroom discussion! None transpired.

In yet another classroom children were obliged to sing a song in mechanical four-four time. There was no similarity between that song and the complex, soaring vocal concert that we heard last night when the Voudon spirits were beckoned.

All around us in abundance was plastic. Plastic cups and dishes for lunch, plastic toys contributed by Americans, plastic dolls and plastic guns.

And canned spaghetti for lunch. The possibility of US profit lurked beneath every surface.

The spark and intelligence to which we were exposed last night were a universe away from what was now before us. Hopefully they were not forever withered in this or in any other Haitian school.

Oh! What if schools were to fling open their doors to Haitian history and art? To Haitian folklore? To Voudon? What if children sang their own songs and wrote their own poetry and what if their own lives were central to the curriculum?

If such were to come about, Haiti might stand a chance of rising again.

Wouldn't it?

Proposal: A teacher-training institute in Haiti encompassing progressive education in cooperation with the most enlightened schools and universities wherever in the world they may exist.

Our food arrived! More anon.

Entry #13 Tuesday, October 12, 2010

Edy, the all-around handy guy who fixes the failing generator every night and then gets the wireless internet connection going, is also the owner of a large, serviceable station wagon and is known locally as the very best of chauffeurs.

I hired him to transport Molly and me to La Vallée— "Lavale"— as it is written in Creole.

The journey from Leogane to Lavale cannot be more than thirty miles but it took us almost three hours. The mountains we crossed were high, the curves precipitous and, once we turned off the main highway at Carrefour St. Antoine and forded the river to make our way along the rutted and rock-strewn Lavale road, progress became imperceptible.

Frankly, the thought of spending the night at CODEHA head-quarters as I had perhaps a dozen times in the past did not appeal to me then. Sleeping on a bulging mattress, sharing a room with someone who snores or who must put up with my own snoring, having to use an insect-ridden outhouse, washing myself in a rusty pan with water collected from the rain ... all this struck me as entirely worthy and enlightening but far better suited to someone of Molly's age than of mine. I am in my eightieth year. She is twenty.

CODEHA is an organization of Lavale and Port au Prince youth. It was founded by "Gody," Godfroy

Boursiquot, a secular, charismatic youth leader. I've known him for some fifteen years.

CODEHA is an acronym for "Corde des Enfants Haitiennes" the meaning of which is that the organization is like a rope bonding all children together and providing them with sufficient collective strength so that there is nothing they cannot accomplish.

One of the many plans in my head is someday, perhaps soon, to organize a visit here of old folks from Kendal in order to view Lavale up close, to participate in some of its activities, and perhaps to become motivated to be sponsors.

It therefore makes sense for me to locate appropriate dining and sleeping quarters for people of my own old, white, flaccid, middle class American sort.

I had remembered that one of the kids some years ago had taken me to check out the Prag Hotel in the Lavale sub-settlement of Ridore which is directly up the mountainside from the CODEHA headquarters which in turn is in the Ridore sub-community of Tuff.

Lavale covers a huge area comprising fourteen sub-settlements. It is more a township than a town.

Molly, Edy and I decided on a spaghetti lunch at the Prag. It was okay. Then I signed in for the night.

Review: Hardly an elegant place but certainly top notch in having running water, flush toilets—located in the halls to be sure—rooms with doors that may be locked, and reasonably comfortable beds.

There are no screens but bugs are few up here in the mountains. However, the cutest little lizard did race cheerfully down a wall and across my floor just before bedtime.

There is only one other guest here. He did not appear for dinner so I ate alone. Edy and Molly wandered off. Elsewhere.

Morning: Edy drove Molly back. We had breakfast together then she and I hiked down the mountain to visit CODEHA headquarters. School children in neat blue uniforms, returning home from their morning sessions raced past us with the speed and certainty of mountain goats. They glanced at us and giggled most likely because we were slow, white and foreign.

Then a batch of high spirited teenage girls materialized. They walked for a while beside us holding our hands. They redirected us politely when we almost missed the turnoff to CODEHA.

We arrived at CODEHA to find everything locked and deserted.

One guy appeared. Jean Paul, a volunteer from the local area who explained that 'Ti Ma, a long time stalwart of CODEHA, was off showing somebody a place to start a hang gliding business and would shortly return. He also said that a woman, a certain Desiree, was in town and would arrive soon.

We waited for what seemed like a very long time. I was concerned that Molly to whom I had described CODEHA as a particularly exciting program, would be disappointed.

Eventually a motorcycle came roaring up the pitted dirt road. A man was driving. Behind him sat a large, young, cheerful woman: The long-awaited Desiree.

Desiree was a full-blown theatrical presence, a musical act of a memorable sort, Mary Poppins as played by Ethel Merman. She spoke loudly and fast, punctuating her sentences with raucous laughter while covering considerable material with each word. She is the sort who leaves her listener far behind, scrambling breathlessly to catch up.

Desiree, a Canadian of mixed ancestry, has the light brown skin and the curly hair of someone with African genes although she claims also to have an Ukrainian background. I wouldn't be surprised if she were part Jewish. Actually, her mother, she later told me, is from Trinidad. Her father is Irish. Desiree speaks English as if it were her first language but claims that her French is even better. She is also entirely comfortable in Spanish. However, she said that she is just a beginner in Haitian Krayole.

She has traveled in many countries, always on a shoestring and an impulse. She landed in Haiti soon after meeting Mme Carolle, a supporter of Gody's in San Diego who told her of the work he is doing. It sounded right up her alley so she hopped a plane and here she is.

"Where are you actually from?" I asked when I first heard her speak.

"San Diego," she said.

"You do look like a Californian," I said, thinking Hollywood.

"What does a Californian look like?" she asked.

"Jewish," I said.

If Desiree impressed me strongly, one can only imagine the effect she must have had on rebellious Molly. Stagestruck, Molly listened and grinned. This was a mentor from heaven.

Desiree has been in Lavale for five months during which time she became passably competent in the language and had a major impact on the CODEHA program. She has been giving music lessons to children, and she organizes song feasts and dramatic performances. She has also taken an active role in the agricultural activities and showed us with pride the section of the garden where bamboo has been planted.

Bamboo has many uses. It is both strong and flexible. As such it can be used as a building material that can mitigate the effects of earthquakes. It grows quickly like a grass but its roots are deep enough to prevent soil erosion, a long time major problem in Haiti.

Desiree also showed us a garden in which what appeared to be a leafy vegetable—the name of which I did not jot down and have forgotten—was planted. This crop, like bamboo, has diverse uses. It can be eaten but it can also be ground into a powder and mixed with water to create a kind of concrete.

We gossiped about Gody with whom she has worked very closely.

Gody, we agreed, is a great and inspiring man who could become president of Haiti if he wished to run. He is a superstar, theatrical and inspiring, able almost instantly have a crowd singing, laughing and united in a sense of community.

Despite her own whoop-de-doo free style, Desiree seems to have a practical mind and, although she receives no salary, she is properly concerned about funding as well as the organizational structure of CODEHA.

I told her of my recommendation that CODEHA become a "development partner" with Fonkoze giving it the capability of offering US donors tax credits. Going that route would be better, I said, than forming an American CODEHA partner. Two reasons, Desiree added: First, it would avoid the paper work and bureaucratic structuring required of tax-exempt organizations. Second, it would benefit from an affiliation with the far better known Fonkoze thus potentially attracting likely donors.

Desiree has a tough, businesslike mind.

Desiree's way of thinking is a necessary corrective to the mental destruction of the young mind that has been accomplished by the Haitian school. Children here are taught that there is only one right answer, only one way to go about doing anything. All one requires is a formula, a map, an instruction booklet which is to be memorized through deadening repetition the end point of which is that the young person becomes trained to obey the orders of those who are in command. Slavery redux.

Voudon represents the opposite, the imagination of the person within the womb of the culture, the socialized longing, the sensuality, the humor, the dizzying leaps of imagination. Liberation.

Desiree enhances the very soul of their own culture to the children of Haiti.

Entry #14 Wednesday, October 13, 2010, A little past 5PM.

Time, as they say, flies: A. Chekhov.

I have only one more day in Lavale. On Friday, Edy will drive me to Port-au-Prince and on Saturday I fly to New York. Sunday, I take a bus to Hanover where Mary and I now live. I am ready.

I have enjoyed my time in Haiti as always but am frustrated that in the face of so many problems and so much readily available talent, little happens to alleviate the misery. In many ways things seem to be getting worse. Especially now, post-earthquake.

After a good night's sleep, a lovely cold shower and a so-so breakfast consisting of a spicy omelette, sweetened orange juice, banana fritters, and all the white bread rolls I could eat, I hiked down the hill to CODEHA headquarters.

The path is very steep and maybe a mile long. It rained last night and the yellow clay path turned slippery. I picked my way down carefully carrying a large bag over my shoulder filled with gifts for CODEHA including a one-person tent, Zutano clothes and dolls, an old but intact cassette recorder, and a couple of small books that I had self-published about Haiti one of which has a Creole text.

Lithe Haitians, children, farmers, and mothers trotted effortlessly by me, all of them wishing me a cheery "good morning" as I labored down the hill and a few offering to help carry my bag. But no. I was okay. I did slip a few times but never actually fell and was justly proud of my achievements.

Little more than fifty yards from the CODEHA community center, stood the great 'Ti Ma, machete in hand. We embraced, said how happy we were to see each other and to inquire about each other's wife and children.

'Ti Ma is a country man, modest, laconic in a universally rural sort of way reminiscent of Vermonters I know. And when he has something to say, it invariably has substance. He is profoundly loyal to his family, his community—the Tuff settlement of Lavale—and he works ceaselessly and selflessly for the betterment of its citizens.

He led me to where he and his family are now living. It is a meager, cluttered shack just across the path from the remnants of the concrete house they had occupied until the earthquake destroyed all but part of its shell. Fortunately, no one was hurt.

This is a house that 'Ti Ma had built with his own hands. Supplies had been purchased thanks to contributions from Vermont. It was one of several monuments to the spirit of solidarity between our state and Lavale, the other being the community center that has become an important focus of CODEHA and all of its programs and events.

'Ti Ma assured me that he will rebuild the house. It was one of the few that were destroyed in Lavale. Lavale survived the earthquake far better than did the cities of Port-au-Prince and Leogane.

Mme Bertha, 'Ti Ma's wife, and I greeted each other with great warmth. They now have four children, three boys and a girl. The youngest, a thirteen month old boy, was on the floor in his baby chair observing us. The next elder, a girl, age three, is in pre-school and the two older boys, seven and eleven are in elementary school. Education for these children was possible only because of a contribution by an American man, a former volunteer, who took an interest in the family.

I laid out the gifts that I had brought them, some for CODEHA and some for the family. The former was basically the tent, a simple one-person affair, that I explained might be offered to visitors. I suggested that Molly might be the first to try it out tonight. I also gave the cassette recorder to CODEHA but in 'Ti Ma's care. He said at once that he would use it to interview children and get down their stories.

'Ti Ma uncharacteristically then proceeded to complain of his financial problems. He works full time for the community—for CODEHA—not for money. He is an expert farmer, generous with his time, the food he produces and with everything at his disposal. His friends and neighbors are more than generous with him in return.

But it is not enough. As with all of us, the cash economy makes harsh demands on him. Not everything can be grown through one's own efforts even when those of one's neighbors are added in. There are certain foods that he must buy in the market.

'Ti Ma takes responsibility for a community motorcycle that must be registered and insured. Clothes must be purchased. Gody has for years promised him that when it becomes possible, he will put 'Ti Ma on salary. But that time has not come. The problem: Gody has no financial resources.

"This is not a good situation," I said. "You should be earning enough money to lead a reasonable life. We must find a way to raise funds for CODEHA so that people without resources will not need to volunteer. There must be a way."

Shortly after this conversation I ran into that new staff member, Desiree, in the CODEHA yard. We got into a discussion about funding. She agreed that lack of money is a huge problem here. Despite all of the great successes locally, and all the international NGOs stationed in Haiti, plus the enormous international sympathy that Haiti has received since the earthquake, very little money has arrived.

Yet everyone in CODEHA continues to work on a voluntary basis no matter how severe their needs may be.

We moved on.

The next big event of the day was sky diving. A certain Simon, showed up. He is a French sportsman currently living in the Dominican Republic and is an accomplished sky diver. Strikes me as a bit of a con artist. He has been hanging around Lavale for some time looking for a site on which to start a sky diving business.

Today he gave a promotion demonstration to the community.

A couple of hundred people arrived in a great field that looks over a particularly spectacular part of the valley. Simon unfurled his parachute and gave two glorious rides. The first was to 'Ti Ma and the second was to Desiree. The sun shone bright and the wind was strong although not fierce. The conditions were perfect. The crowds cheered when each of them was carried aloft and again when they landed.

Oh! Imagine Lavale were it to become the center of a sport like that! Imagine the tourist business! Imagine the river of dollars! Imagine ....

This evening at the hotel I was unwinding from an exhausting day, munching my dinner of goat meat, rice, beans, and banana fritters when I heard the mumble of a motorcycle engine in the yard.

"They have come for me," I thought.

Sure enough in walked 'Ti Ma with a man he introduced as the new "Gerant Responsable"—manager—of CODEHA. His duties were unclear. The four of us continued the discussions about money and organization that seems to have been the theme of the day. Although CODEHA is doing better than ever, its needs are increasing and, without adequate funding, the toll on the entire organization has become intolerable. It is not only 'Ti Ma who is having a hard time of it.

We considered various possible funding options including the recruitment of groups of good-willed, wealthy retirees to come here as a workshop to gain an understanding of what is being done to turn this economy around and how they might help.

But that strategy, although it might be successful, would only work episodically. What is needed is a product or a service that might find a market and that stands a chance of bringing in a predictable and solid income.

Thunder and lightning were in the air and coming closer. We decided to continue our conversation tomorrow at four in the afternoon. Perhaps Desiree and others will join us.

I need to sleep. Fe do-do as one says in these parts.

Entry #15 Thursday, October 14, My Last Day in Lavale

It is funny how things happen in Lavale, maybe in all of Haiti, too, including Port-au-Prince. Perhaps that's the way of the world. Random encounters lead to interesting possibilities. You just run into people and something may come of it, good as well as bad. Random encounters are the fuel of life.

I went to Western Union this morning to trade another hundred dollars to Gourdes. I think I am doing okay money-wise. The five hundred dollars that I brought along will probably get me through despite the luxury of hiring private cars for travel between cities, something I would never think of doing in Haiti in the old days . . . when I was young.

I sat for a moment on the steps of the Community Bank trying once again to figure out the money system when a well-dressed woman approached and asked where I am from.

"The United States," I said. "But where exactly?" she persisted. "I have been to the United States several times and know something of its geography.".

She had visited Florida and New York, mostly Queens, but had no knowledge of either New Hampshire or Vermont. Her name is Claudette Hilaire. She is the founder and director of a small women's organization based in Lavale's hospital. It is called "PROFASEH" an awkward French acronym that stands for a phrase meaning, "Promotion of Families and Women in Society in the South East of Haiti."

We did not have time to talk very much. She was on her way to open her office at the hospital. I accompanied her.

I learned very little about her or her work but I came away from our encounter with the sense that this was an important contact for future volunteer groups. I took her card and she took mine. Cards are very useful outside of the US.

Yesterday afternoon I met Narline Boursiquot, Gody's cousin once-removed, a girl I had known since she was thirteen and who was now twenty-seven. She came up to me in the street and gave me a big hug as I was chatting with CODEHA people.

We were very happy to see each other. I had known her grandmother, "Gran' Rita," Gody's first cousin, who died three years ago. She was a marvelous peasant woman who was a major presence in the community.

Narline and her sisters, Enid and Marie-Michelle, lived with Gran' Rita and sometimes her brother, Makise, lived there, too. I knew them all. They had another brother and sister from other parts of Haiti who visited from time to time but I barely knew them.

Narline has graduated university in Port au Prince with a degree in education. I am confident that she has the makings of a terrific teacher but she has not been able to find a job. She scrapes by, dividing her time between Port-au-Prince and Lavale where she stays in Gran' Rita's old house. Maybe if we can get something educational going here we can find a job for Narline.

As I made my way back down to the hotel this morning after changing today's cash. I noticed how clean the street was, doubtless swept by earnest young girls. The flowers along the way were in bloom and the valley below was stunning in its extravagant beauty.

I thought of the second dream I had before making this trip, the one about Haiti being more than okay, still lovely, still promising.

I thought, "that was a dream that foretells the future."

Entry #16 Friday, October 15, 2010—The Sister's School, Back to Port au Prince and ... home.

It is early morning. In an hour or so Edy, the guy who drove me from Leogane, will be picking me up to take me to Port-au-Prince. Tomorrow, Saturday, I will be on the afternoon plane to New York, spend one night there and on Sunday will board a bus to Hanover and the sweet, loving arms of Mary and Kendal, the benign old folks home where all our needs and wishes are happily satisfied.

Molly will join me as far as Leogane. She will probably return to Lavale after a few weeks where she plans to remain until May or—who knows?—perhaps .. for the rest of her life.

It has been a fine three days in this town—plus the additional seven in other fine Haitian venues. I will miss all of it—especially the people—but now I am ready to go home.

'Ti Ma asked me when I plan on coming back. "I don't know," I said. "Maybe in a year or two or maybe never."

"Never?" he said, "Why never?"

"I am an old guy," I said.

* * *

Yesterday was another good one and a fitting end to the adventure. Desiree met me as we had agreed at the front of my hotel, Le Prag, at 11:30. She had Molly in tow plus 'Ti Ma and Toussaint—the guy 'Ti Ma introduced to me the other night as the new manager of CODEHA, "le gerant responsable."

Both were on motorcycles. Much conversation followed, indeed a day of conversation beginning as we made up our way to the "Sister's School," an elementary and secondary Catholic girls' institution where Desiree was to teach two classes in music, a remarkable development in this country because, although everybody in this country seems remarkably musical, music education as such is not known to be part of the curriculum anywhere though an integral part of life.

Molly and I waited in the yard while Desiree talked with the principal, a smiling nun wearing an antique blue and white habit. Hundreds of girls were standing about at recess. All were in uniform, blue skirt and white blouse in keeping with the Sister's clothing. Some were running here and there but most were memorizing lessons by repeating them out loud to themselves. This was a traditional Haitian school.

Girls gathered shyly around us, staring and smiling uncertainly. "They probably have never seen a white woman before," Desiree, referring to Molly, suggested, "certainly not one with blond hair. Nor," she added, "an old white guy."

I grinned back at the kids, slapping palms with those who came close and poking an occasional little one on the nose.

They were becoming more relaxed and curious. We were by then surrounded by a great throng, probably over a hundred.

A lot anyway. For all I knew it may have been thousands.

It was time for Desiree's first class. Desiree, followed closely by Molly and a pack of high energy girls, made their way en masse to the classroom.

I came next surrounded by throngs of giggling children of all sizes. Not all were girls. Several boys were among them.

It was a large class, somewhere around forty students, each assigned a desk that was fixed in place. Even before everyone was seated, Desiree began. She is a great performer as well as the sort who delights in carrying on witty dialogs with her audience. Banter and jokes come easily to her. She laughs freely and now and then breaks into hearty guffaws.

The children could not get enough of her. The more she said, the more they said and the more they said, the more she laughed, and the more she laughed, the more she carried the high spirited children along with her.

189

Yet she was strict in her own way. When two girls showed up to class ten minutes late, she greeted them with a Creole song she made up on the spot. My rough translation:

"You are late! You are late! It is not good to be late!"

At once everyone joined in, singing raucously and clapping in rhythm. The two culprits were far from offended. They sang, laughed and clapped along with everyone else.

The subject of the day was a categorization of all of the instruments that may be found in an orchestra— piano, violin, cello, horns, drums, and so on. The idea was to decide what list to put each in: wind, strings, percussion or brass.

Desiree, as I have indicated, has the makings of a great teacher but the exercise was intentionally silly. Some of the instruments were viewed as fitting in more than one category. An accordion, for example: She convinced the kids to call it a "percussion instrument" but the sound as we know is made by wind ... and who really cares?

The main thing is that here in a conventional Haitian Catholic girl's school she brought the kids wonderfully alive. She gave her full attention to them and they gave theirs to her and everyone adored every minute of it.

Then Desiree led another class, considerably larger than the first.

This session drew to a wowser of a conclusion with children coming up to the front to sing a song or tell a riddle. Desiree got a bunch of relatively shy boys to beat drum-surrogates by banging on their desks. The rhythms were convincingly Voudon—at least to my uneducated ear. Desiree joined them by slapping on her own desk while wiggling her body in a distinctly un-nunlike manner.

At the grandest moment of the grand finale Molly did a break dance.

Then I led everyone in song, "Sweetly Sings the Donkey at the Break of Day." The kids especially loved the "He haw, he haw, he haw, he haw, he haw." They continued braying donkey-like as they rushed down the hall at the close of the school day.

Finally, Desiree, Molly, Toussaint, 'Ti Ma and I retreated to a restaurant for a beer and to process what had happened. We agreed that the performance suggested many things that CODEHA could and should do, not merely raise money—although that is certainly important—but to make a significant difference to Haitian education ... and to life. Desiree is, as I have said, a treasure. And putting her together with the many immensely talented children in this community is the formula for an unique version of a liberal education ... whatever that may mean.

Having been in the Sister's School, Toussaint suggested that we stroll down the street to the Brothers'—or "Monks"'— School where he teaches. This is one that the refugee children from Port-au-Prince have been attending since the earthquake. Initially it was local high schoolers who worked with them but soon the Brothers opened their doors to full instructional involvement.

It was a clean, conventional-seeming place. But I was pleasantly surprised to see smatterings of children's art—very little actually—on the walls.

Rain suddenly arrived in large, steady droplets. Jackson, a young motorcycle chauffeur extra-ordinaire, 'Ti Ma and Tous-saint drove us down the slippery mountain on the back of their machines to CODEHA headquarters for a dinner prepared by Madame Maggie Gabrielle, a local woman who loves to cook for CODEHA and is very good at it.

We gave her the old "Hip Hip Hooray!" which she clearly appreciated.

Simon, the French sky diver who is living in the Dominican Republic, joined us. The dinner was supposed to have been the venue for more conversation about programs and fund raising but it turned into a farewell party for Molly me. All very convivial. Molly is going back to Leogane tomorrow. I will join her that far and then I will head to Port au Prince alone. And then the States.

I am now in Port-au-Prince in the same guest house where I stayed a week ago, the one that caters to Protestant missionary do-gooders.

I have been stand-offish. But today I met a couple of teachers from Canada and a husband and wife team from Spain. The latter are with something called "Psychologists Beyond Borders." They have been working in the tent cities not so much doing therapy as training social workers. That's fine, I thought.

But I myself am preoccupied with Haitian resilience which impresses me as exceptional and more promising. Who needs psychologists?

Anthropologists might even make more sense. Maybe.

"Haitians are very resilient," the husband psychologist said. "They got over the trauma of the earthquake in only a month. There is no trauma in the population any more."

"And what statistics have you gathered?" the wife psychologist asked.

"None," I said. "I make up fanciful stories."

Part VI

Abuse!?

Sunday, October 17th.

I am traveling on the Amtrak "Vermonter."

We just pulled out of Hartford. Another four and a half hours to White River Junction where Mary will meet me, then to dinner and home in our dear sweet retirement community, our geezerly ghetto.

There are many thoughts about the visit to Haiti that are rattling around my head.

There was the time that Carla drove me down the Delmas hill to Wall's Guest House. I suggested that we stop at St. Joseph's Home for Boys, the first orphanage I knew in Haiti. I had heard that it had been destroyed by the earthquake.

Carla agreed.

We turned right at Delmas 97 making our way past the piles of rubble that had been homes, some of them rather nice, middle class places. St. Joseph's Home for Boys was once a structure of four stories. Most of it was now flat to the ground. A small part of the first story remained.

It was sad to look on this destruction. I was flooded by memories, largely pleasant ones, but they were clouded by worrisome confusion and distaste.

The founder and director of the place a certain Michael Geilenfeld, is an affable, well-spoken fellow. Michael came to Haiti some thirty years earlier as a young American monk in an order affiliated with Mother Theresa's operation. He began his service by working with homeless boys in a small, informal group. They slept and ate together huddled under trees and awnings and in abandoned buildings. Heroic work.

Michael asked the Order to allow him to buy a building of his own so that he could open an orphanage. But Mother Theresa did not allow him that. He therefore raised the necessary funds independently through personal connections, withdrew from Mother Theresa's Order and opened his orphanage.

It was probably an odd sort of place from the start consistent with Michael's liberal religious vision. It soon became well known among well-intentioned Americans including myself.

Its oddness lay in the fact that while it was indeed an orphanage, it was also a guest house and as such provided visitors with nice beds, clean rooms and good food all at a reasonable price. The orphan boys served as staff.

Michael was an excellent host. His orphanage became the place of choice for educated foreigners; a bridge to Haiti for scholars, journalists, missionaries, myriad do-gooders and people of a wide range of political persuasions.

And Michael's efforts and personal charm attracted funds that were used for operating the enterprise.

Prayers were regular and frequent—morning, evening and at special times on holidays. Discussions of religious matters often took place as well.

Michael also promoted Haitian art. He gathered and maintained an impressive collection that adorned the walls. The orphanage in fact resembled a museum more than a home although the boys did keep a pet parrot plus a dog and Michael employed an excellent Haitian cook.

St. Joseph's indeed became a cultural mecca, far from the hand-to-mouth days from whence it arose.

The boys seemed loyal to Michael. They appeared to appreciate all he had done for them.

The building was large but did not house a large population, perhaps thirty boys at a time. All of them attended school in the community and were given an opportunity to learn classical ballet and Haitian folk dance classes at a school nearby. Some of the boys became very accomplished.

The troupe made regular tours of the American midwest where Michael originated. The boys' performances generated operating money for the orphanage and in so doing added to their sense of self-worth.

Michael regularly expanded his enterprise. Every few years a new floor was added to the building. When I last visited several years ago, it had four. On the very top was a chapel.

Michael also founded affiliate orphanages. One, still functioning despite reported damage, is called, "Wings of Hope." It is for handicapped children and is located in the town of Fermath on the mountainside above Petionville. Another is in the city of Jacmel. I do not know if either still stands. Both were operated by graduates of St. Joseph's in accordance with Michael's vision.

I very much admired what Michael was able to do even though his vision was different in many respects from my own.

Yet there were things about him that bothered me. His religion, studiously pious, rang with Hallmark card sentimentality.

What made me far more uncomfortable had to do with unrelated matters. They was hard to put my finger on. There were often, for example, older white women hanging around, mothering sorts, who seemed to worship Michael, outdoing each other to be helpful. No big deal ... but notable.

More concerning: There appeared an occasional, adult Haitian guy wandering about who did not seem to be affiliated with the place. One of these in particular struck me as theatrically homosexual in appearance and manner.

I never knew Michael to be in an unambiguous or even a suggestive love relationship with either a woman or a man. He was social in his manner but fundamentally a loner. Nonetheless, St. Joseph's Home reeked, in its way, with a distinctly sexual scent.

Michael appeared gay. So what? So do lots of people.... I am

not inclined to be prejudiced.

Businesslike but informal, describes Michael's style. While helpful to the boys in the sense of feeding, housing and educating them, he seemed at the same time stand-offish, as generous but cool, as compelling in his manner rather than seductive or authoritarian. I think of him as a sociable loner, a thoughtful host and a good businessman.

Then as if out of the blue came the accusations and the publicity.

On a dance tour to the American midwest in the early '90s, several of Michael's boys asked Michigan Social Services for asylum on the grounds that he had abused them sexually. The asylum requests were granted.

The news made the papers both in Detroit and Port-au-Prince. They caused quite a stir in the latter, I understand.

Several years after that another group of boys made a similar claim but this time they were denied US asylum.

Haitian authorities investigated Michael but did nothing, giving him a de facto clean bill of health. He was also investigated by an American court. Again: No guilty verdict.

Yet the word about Michael on the Haitian street was not good. Neighbors I spoke with—a sample of about a half dozen—claimed to know that he was a sexual predator.

Although allegations were common, hard data was rare; difficult to find or nonexistent. Michael denied everything. He maintained that the appeals for asylum were a function simply of the attractiveness to poor boys from the streets of America's great wealth.

Some Haiti-based US clergy remained clear of him. He was not part of their circle. A leading nun I spoke with was strongly critical of him. She believed the rumors. And a knowledgeable orphanage director I liked and trusted, a Haitian, told me that she had always known that he molested his boys.

I interviewed some of the oldest and most articulate of Michael's boys. A representative answer: "He never bothered me personally and I don't know what he may have done to other kids but whatever might have been bad was not as important as the good he did. If not for him I would have been dead on the streets a long time ago."

Because of its black population, extreme and chronic poverty, Haiti has long been a favored venue for white, male, sexual predators to find and exploit sex partners; some favor children of either gender, some only females. Some only males.

It was sad to view the remnants of the orphanage. Utter destruction. I learned that none of the boys got hurt and that is a "blessing" as Michael would say.

Would he also say that the destruction itself was God's work?

* * *

Carla drove her car a bit too close to what remained of the building. Her front and rear wheels both skidded off the curb and lodged themselves in the mud. I thought that we were stuck there for good. But eight young men who were hanging around nearby, noticed us. They had not been part of the orphanage. But they knew Carla and held her in high regard. Together they pushed and shoved and after no more than a few minutes had us on the road again.

In Haiti at its best—and Vermont as well—no one asks for anything nor expects anything in return. Digging us out was simply an act of friendship and human decency. It was what anybody would do without giving it a thought.

We take care of each other.

Part IV

Russia!

My Russian Family
1992

Yesterday afternoon there was a great party at Mark and Olya's house. An amazing spread of food and drink; much vodka, endless toasts, animated conversations, a delighted viewing of photographs of the family, going back some eighty years.

It was family. My family. Cousins. Some remarkably close.

Present were Rafik and Genya, children of Fanya and Solomon Ariel. Fanya was a daughter of Isaak Golom-stock, a brother to my Grandma Tamara. Rafik's children were there, two young men, twins, Georgi and Andrei.

Andrei speaks English fluently and pretty much took me over for the duration of the party.

Genya's son, Stanislav, was there, too. He's a body builder. He wondered if there were body builders on the American side of the family.

Lisa, the daughter of Sasha, the KGB general in charge of "inspecting" (supervising?) the GULAG, was present as well. Through Andrei, I asked Lisa a number of questions about her father that she answered freely.

He fought in the revolution and remained in the Red Army, rising to the rank of general. In 1937 he was transferred to the KGB. He did not choose the assignment. His rank was lowered in the secret police. Jews under Stalin it seems were often placed in potentially unpopular offices. If the public were to become outraged or even somewhat less than supportive, Jews were blamed.

The family actually lived in the Kremlin. Lisa went to school there. One of her classmates was Maxim Litvinoff's daughter. There were in fact two Kremlin schools operating, one more elite than the other. Svetlana Stalin went to the more elite one. Lisa knew her although she went to the one less elite.

Sasha was thrown out of the KGB in 1951. During his last years, Stalin who wanted a constant "turnover" of personnel, executed most of his closest officers, those who knew him best. It was a miracle that Sasha was not also murdered. He used to stay awake at night, Lisa said, head in hands, expecting a knock at the door at any moment. This constant terror had severe effects on his health. He suffered three heart attacks. He died in 1968 of the last of these three.

Although around the time of the Revolution most Jews were social democrats rather than Bolsheviks, many came to support the new Soviet regime because it promised full citizenship to Jews and an end to anti-Semitism. But it was this hopeful enthusiasm that became the basis of Soviet anti-Semitism. In the minds of many Russians, Stalin was blamed on the Jews.

It was hard to inquire into all this as much as I would have liked because, after all, it was a party for me. Also: My Russian was less than basic.

Andrei, however, spoke English well. He told me about his engineering business, his trips as a hydroelectricity consultant to Australia and Indonesia and his conviction that to survive these times, one had to make one's "own" economy. Among other things, Andrei had become a tour guide for Moscow, a city he knows very well and loves. A number of people I have met in this country love their cities whether St. Petersburg, Moscow or Ekaterininberg.

In a fit of alcoholic enthusiasm, I attempted a witty toast. Everybody at the party obviously hated the Communists. So: "Na Marksa!" I shouted,—"To Marx!"—weaving, vodka glass in hand.

Cold silence from the entire gathering.

"Groucho Marxists!" I yelled, gagging on my laughter.

The silence deepened.

Hmmmm. I had imagined that Russians knew all about American culture.

Andrei asked me to explain what I had tried to say. "Groucho, you know, Groucho," I said, "the guy with the mustache and the glasses. The funny walk." I demonstrated. "Oh," said Andrei, "you mean Grooocho!" He passed this information on to the group. Polite laughter. "Heh heh heh heh heh."

Somebody then told a real joke. A man goes to hell and finds Beria up to his neck in blood. "How do you manage?" Beria is asked. "I am standing on the shoulders of our Great Comrade, Joseph Stalin," he replies.

Okay.

It appears that people at least in this portion of our extended family are living well enough.

Yuri and Masha have a nice apartment, two television sets (one old), and lots of books and knick knacks, to say nothing of Nikusha, the Airedale, who cost them almost three thousand rubles—a month's wage. (And they claim to be typical urban Russians).

Note: Unlike in America where we have special dog food, in Russia dogs eat table scraps. Nikusha, it seems, doesn't touch his kasha. All he will eat is meat. He doesn't care if it's fresh or processed like kielbasa, Yuri stands on long lines at the Unimarkt, the spare cooperative "supermarket," just for good, old Nik.

It's true that Yuri and Masha live in a housing project. And the halls are crumbling and saturated with the stale odor of darkness. But the apartments themselves in such places—judging from the four I have thus far visited in this country—Galya's, Nina's, Yuri and Masha's, and Mark and Olya's—are all quite pleasant and very well cared for. There is little fear of thievery or assault. Although Masha and Yuri have two locks on their front door, they normally use neither. The situation here is quite unlike what is to be found in American public housing.

I told Yuri that in most American housing projects people cannot own pets. "How come?" Yuri asked. "It's your apartment, you should be allowed to have anything you want in it."

Mark seems to be doing well. Brilliantly, in fact. He informed me that he has three hundred-forty employees working for him. He owns two cars personally, one for him and one for his wife, Olya. A third is for his business. He lives in a large comfortable apartment—big even by U. S. standards. And he owns a new Panasonic television set, a VCR, a camcorder ... and so on.

His business as near as I can tell includes three stores, several houses and a construction operation.

He also supplies construction materials to other contractors.

Everyone—Mark, Yuri and Masha—have the convenience of being able to walk to work. Many people own dachas. Four to six weeks vacation during the summer is standard. Despite egregious problems with the system, medical care remains free.

However, people do worry. A lot.

Masha has had a serious heart condition for twenty years. Somehow it's connected with her salivary glands. She pointed to them trying to explain the problem to me.

Rafik is an invalid. He's had several strokes. He used to work in the same institute as his two sons, Georgei and Andrei. They are all engineers with a specialty in hydroelectrics.

Rafik left his wife when the boys were young. He went on to other women. Masha thinks the's had three or four wives in all.

Neither Mark, Georgi nor Andrei have been raised as Jews but, according to the passports they carry, their "nationality" is Jewish. All Russians have a "nationality." And all Russians must carry internal passports with them at all times. However, currently there is talk of doing away with such things.

Andrei is not married. He's had two major but disastrous love affairs. Mark and Georgi have both married non-Jews. Indeed Mark married a total of two Russians and Georgi married a Georgian. All three young men are interested in learning more about their Jewish roots.

I suspect that Georgi drinks too much. He continued making toasts after everyone but me had lost interest.

I raised yet another toast: "May the Russian economy improve enough to allow all of you to visit America soon."

Andrei snapped back: "We wont depend on the Russian economy. We shall make our own economy!"

He and Mark, probably Georgi, too, have done exactly that. For all I know, it may even have been achieved within the constraints of the law.

Evia Kroshka

I am going to take a couple kids off on a spring outing today. They are from "Dietsky Priut Almusa"—The Almus Children's Shelter. It is in St. Petersburg, Russia. I am currently living at Almus as a guest, a sort of resident grand-pa. We will be going to a street circus workshop. It is to take place at "The Lazaret Punkt." I suspect that means "The Lazaret Neighborhood."[7]

I've been living in the Dietsky Priut Almusa for almost two weeks and having a great time. The children call me "Dyedushka Bob," Grandpa Bob.

A girl and a boy, energetic Lehrer and tiny, muscular Serogia, were chosen by the vospitatilye—child care workers—to join me to the street circus because, in deference to me, they are relatively easy kids to manage.

Both children are nine. But Serogia looks younger. Lehrer smiles easily; Serogia, serious, and silent, often wears a pained expression.

We took a bus, then the Metro, to the Vostannia Voksal (Station); finally a cab to the apartment

---

[7]My translations from the Russian require verification.

where we thought the circus workshop was to take place. But no one was there. We hung out, wondering what to do.

Eventually, Natalia Nikolaevna arrived. She is middle-aged, thin, businesslike; a commanding presence, small but but seeming much larger. She was dressed in a stark

black sweater and skirt. She stood erect. Accompanying her was a tiny, brown, very lively probable Poodle, obviously ideal for a circus. Its name was Evia Kroshka.

"Kroshka," Natalia Nikolaevna explained, "means a crust of bread. Evia means nothing. It is just a cute name for a cute little girl."

Natalia Nikolaevna explained that the street circus program, begun and initially funded by a German student organization, has recently fallen on hard times. In fact, there is now only enough money remaining for two more months.

Natalia Nikolaevna herself has been paid so little— five hundred rubles or the equivalent of about fifteen dollars a month—that she has been obliged to look around for another job.

The program, then, is now effectively out of business but children do continue to show up for rehearsals. The reason, she explained, that only one local child plans to come today is that it is a holiday, Russian Easter. I hadn't remembered that.

Holiday or not, Natalia Nikolaevna worked for over an hour with Serogia and Lehrer. Soon after they began, the young girl from the neighborhood appeared and joined them.

Natalia Nikolaevna is a tough instructor, theatrically authoritarian. Yet the children took to her and were eager to win her approval. She soon had them jumping through hoops, performing summersaults, flips, and back arches.

Serogia was good at everything, by far the best of the three. The local girl was there for only her fourth time, she told us, but already was quite competent although not nearly as graceful as Serogia—who curiously never lost his pained look.

Lehrer, at first tentative, soon threw herself into the activity and sparkled. She learned to do a passable summersault.

Then Natalia Nikolaevna demonstrated the skills of her little dog, Evia Kroshka, much to everyone's delight.

Afterwards, I took the kids for a lunch treat at a blini fast food restaurant, a McDonald's-like place called Skaska, "fairy tale."

The children had never been to a restaurant before and didn't know how to order. But they soon got the hang of it and stuffed themselves. Serogia ordered a monstrous portion of ice cream for desert. Lehrer bought chewing gum, enough to share, she said, with her friends back at the priut.

Two days later:

Natalia Nikolaevna is coming this afternoon to Priut Almus with Evia Kroshka, her probable Poodle—at my invitation.

I met Natalia Nikolaevna and Evia Kroshka at the Lomonosovskaya Metro station and accompanied them to the priut.

Evia Kroshka was in Natalia Nikolaevna's arms but as soon as we emerged from the station, Natalia Nikolaeva placed her on the sidewalk. Immediately a crowd gathered.

Evia Kroshka was dressed in a pretty red jacket and matching skirt complete with a purple ribbon. She wore a small brown hat and in her mouth carried a blue plastic bucket for donations.

I placed a one-ruble coin in the bucket. Immediately fifty or more coins landed beside it. People fell all over themselves to throw in money for Evia Kroshka. Who can say how long or hard these people worked to earn it?

Natalia Nikolaevna then had Evia Kroshka do a series of clever tricks much to the squeals of the crowd, children and grownups alike—including me.

Evia Kroshka barked five times in response to the five fingers that Natalia Nikolaevna held up to her. Then two barks for two fingers.

"Time for a nap," Natalia Nikolaevna said. Evia Kroshka rolled over immediately and went to sleep on command.

Through all of this Natalia Nikolaevna kept up a running commentary. It must have been witty because everyone roared with laughter.

As we left, giggling children ran after us with still more coins to throw in the bucket.

Back at the priut, all the children gathered in the "Sports Hall," a gymnasium on the first floor where Natalia Nikolaevna and Evia Kroshka put on a repeat performance.

Everyone laughed and applauded.

Then Natalia Nikolaevna taught acrobatic tricks to whomever was interested. Eight year old Katya, a kid I didn't know, performed a most remarkable split. But Serogia remained the most supple of anyone.

Later when the vospitatalye—child care workers— gathered with Natalia Nikolaevna and me in the staff kitchen for tea, soup, cake and gossip, I said, "Natalia Nikolaevna, you and Evia Kroshka are a world class team!"

Some days after the visit, curious about Serogia, I invited him and a few of his friends to draw pictures for me. I had come to Russia equipped with crayons and paper donated by Ben and Jerry's ice cream company.

The other kids drew expected things such as fields, trees and sunshine. But Serogia drew war, darkness and fire; planes bombing and bombs exploding. Tanks. Dead bodies. Utter destruction.

My Russian language skills were not adequate to attempt an interview but I did manage a few awkward words to indicate that his message was well received.

I also gave him a hug which he accepted ... although with evident discomfort.

An Interview with Mikhail Makarievich-"Makarich"

Director of Priut Almus[8]
(where Serogia and Lehrer live)

We founded Priut Almus in 1991 just after the collapse of the Soviet Union. The situation in Leningrad—St. Petersburg—and throughout Russia was very bad then. The political collapse led to severe difficulties in the financial sector and, beyond that, in the family. There was a sudden increase in deep poverty especially as it impinged on the upbringing of children.

Local authorities were open to ideas them about how to solve these problems. They were particularly interested in creating a system to protect the rights of children. A network of experimental institutions and organizations emerged for that purpose.

Only dietskiy doma—orphanages—and internatye—public boarding schools—existed before that. Priutye—drop-in centers—could be found in Russia prior to the Revolution but not under

---

[8]For background, see: Tales of Priut Almus, Participant Observation in a Russian Children's Shelter, iUniverse, 2009

the Soviets. Priutye have now returned to a limited, temporary degree but are viewed with suspicion by the authorities probably because enrollment is voluntary rather than police or court-ordered. It is up to the child and/or the family. An unaccompanied child can come to our door, seek refuge and be given it as family resources are sought.

But after one year, a child must have a permanent placement either with his or her original family, a foster family, and or a dietskiy dom. But not with the priut in which he or she may now happily reside. I often try to negotiate with the authorities for a longer stay. Sometime I am successful but often I result merely in antagonizing them.

While it is true that orphanages, shelters and group homes for children have existed in the West for some time, it may be that Almus is different from each of them in significant respects that I am not aware of.

Priut Almus grew from my own history and experiences. My dietskiy dom was not a bad place. I have many good memories of it. Best of all, it was located right in the middle of Leningrad in the Smolny District, an historic, well-favored neighborhood. The high culture of the city surrounded us and, as luck would have it, my dietskiy dom did not have its own school but rather sent us to the local district school that happened to be one of the best in the city. There we received a real education.

Most other dietskiy doma residents were not so fortunate. There is normally little of educational value that exists beyond the walls of most institutions for children. Residents sit alone with their problems and have no prospect of being exposed to culture, the outdoors, the life of the mind, the imagination, or any resources that might lead them to a life beyond their sadness.

The government supported our dietskiy dom and the district school with the required necessities including food, clothes, and so on. But resources overall were extremely limited at the time. There were no extras. This, you see, was immediately after the Second World War. Yet somehow funds were found to send us to camp each summer. The government did as well by us as it could. At the same time, we were deprived of those less tangible things that are necessary for every child, a real home and the realization that somebody needs you and that you need them.

Some of us found ways to compensate. We discovered that on our own initiative we could become engaged in interesting after-school activities. Our city had a great deal to offer even during that difficult time. I myself was drawn to theater. I came to love theater passionately. It became my salvation.

Memories of my childhood, despite living in an institution, are rather pleasant. In some ways I had a rich, emotionally satisfying life. For example, my dietskiy dom did not prevent me from attending a neighborhood theater club. I am forever grateful for having had such an opportunity. Many children experience nothing similar.

In Almus, children are given as much cultural exposure as we can provide. We take them to museums, concerts, the circus, and all manner of cultural events.

The saddest times I remember in the dietskiy dom were the Parent Days when children were allowed to visit with their relatives, whether grandparents, aunts and uncles, and, if the had them, mothers and fathers. These took place on weekends, holidays or vacations.

Not all children were fortunate enough to have somebody come for them. The most terrible feeling is the loneliness, the sense of being neglected. On Parent Days you stood by a very tall window looking out at the street below, waiting, waiting, waiting for someone to come, someone who would take you with them. But no one comes. I can still remember that desperate loneliness.

Can you imagine a still worse scenario—a child who not only has no one but also has no hobby to compensate, no favorite thing to do, no experiences to draw on, nothing to read, nothing to stimulate the imagination, no way to escape? It is dreadful. Such a child will have problems for his or her entire life.

The image of the lonely child by the window has haunted me for years. During Soviet times, such a child had only the possibility of a dietskiy dom or an internat but today there are other resources. Children who watch at the window now might be welcomed into foster families, group homes, priutye and so on. At Almus, we offer children as many interesting activities as we can, the possibility of choice and the likelihood of being treated as a person, as an individual human being.

Our vosplitatilye—child care workers—assume surrogate parental functions but they of necessity are time-limited. But no matter where the long-term placement may be, many children manage to return here to a visit.

Almus is supported by the City of St. Petersburg and provincial governments.

Unfortunately, we do not have the resources to support follow-up studies.

* * *

Ousted!

Dr. Roman Yorick, Director of Doctors of the World, St. Petersburg, sent me an email today, November 7, 20. 08. It read in part:

"Mikhail Makarievich was quite hastily and unhappily retired by the authorities a couple of weeks ago."

* * *

And the priut was shut down.

Makarich was deeply anti-authoritarian but oddly authoritarian in his free-thinking. He was famously a thorn in the side of bureaucrats. An example: a priut could legally retain a child for no more than one year. Beyond that children needed to be adopted or placed in an orphanage. Makarich, believing that his dropin center should be a home, argued for extended retention intelligently, vociferously and often. He had a mixed record of success, sometimes winning, sometimes losing but invariably antagonizing the bureaucracy.

Svetlana—"Sveta"—Konstantinova, translator of the Makarich interview, is a cultured, self contained woman who had a lot to say in her own voice. But she is a disciplined professional—a woman of the theater and a teacher of English. And did not permit her personal views to interrupt the flow of our conversation.

As a child, Sveta acted in the Leningrad Children's Theater under Makarich's direction.

"Makarich is a very great man," she said.

"And my best Russian mentor," I said.

"I see some of myself in him," I mumbled under my breath.

Thank You

To everyone mentioned in this book

And to countless others

Plus five dogs

And two donkeys

But mostly to Mary, my lodestar

Bob

Robert Belenky, a clinical child psychologist, has worked in children's camps, schools, communities and institutions.

He developed a retreat center in Vermont for children and families.

On retirement, Bob began a series of visits to Haiti and Russia to learn at close range how young people may be helped to grow up when natural families are unavailable.

Bob has written several books, and has taught at Harvard, Boston College, Boston University, Goddard College and Concordia University.

Bob and his wife, Mary, have two children, five grandchildren, and one gifted dog.